THE BIOSOCIAL NATURE OF MAN

The Biosocial Nature of Man

by ASHLEY MONTAGU

GROVE PRESS, INC.
New York
EVERGREEN BOOKS LTD.
London

136
A s 3 b

4 2 / 2 0

To

Theodosius Dobzhansky

CONTENTS

PREFACE

In this little book I have attempted to deal with some of the questions which must be asked if one is to gain some understanding of the nature of human nature. The two most important of these questions are: (1) How much of the biological enters into the making of human nature? and (2) How much of the social experience of the individual enters into the making of that nature? Hence, the title of this book. No one is, of course, in a position to answer these questions completely. What I have tried to do in the present volume is to clarify the issues, to set down the relevant facts as scientists have come to know them, and to examine some of the representative theories concerning the biosocial nature of man.

Goethe once remarked that where an idea is wanting a word can always be found to take its place. In the area of discussion with which this book is concerned—human nature—words, alas, have too often passed for ideas.

Understanding and correcting the erroneous meanings incorporated in such words as "heredity," "environment," "constitution," and "human nature," are not merely matters of semantic interest, but are of vital importance for the welfare of humanity. *The Biosocial Nature of Man* is humbly offered to the reader as a contribution toward the achievement of that welfare.

Princeton,   ASHLEY MONTAGU
New Jersey

INTRODUCTION

Aristotle described man as a political animal, thus hitting off in a phrase his essential characteristics, namely, that he is at once an animal and a social creature in a rather special sense—a biosocial creature. All animals are social creatures, that is they are both living organisms and interact with each other to confer mutually beneficial advantages upon one another, but man as an animal and as a social creature is unique in several respects. As an animal, man is the most plastic, the most adaptable, the most educable, of all living creatures. Indeed, the single trait which is alone sufficient to distinguish man from all other creatures is the quality of *educability—it* is *the species* character of *Homo sapiens.*

As a social organism man is the most complexly developed of all social organisms. In fact, the difference which characterizes the societies which are peculiar to nonhuman animals and that which characterizes human social life is so great and complex, that the difference may, in effect, be considered one of kind rather than degree of development. The difference lies in the cultural capacities and their development in man as com-

pared with the virtual nonexistence of these capacities
in nonhuman creatures. The full understanding of the
meaning of this difference is of the greatest importance
for mankind, for the failure to realize the meaning of
this difference has led to much confusion in discussions
of the biosocial nature of man; and, what is worse, in
the recent history of world civilization, this confusion
has had the most disastrous effects. Man is an animal;
but he is also a great deal more than that, he is a human
animal, a culture-making creature, the creature who
is capable of transcending all animality—and is in
danger of descending to a perverted animal level when
he forgets that fact.

Theories spun by men desirous of rationalizing their
otherwise unjustifiable conduct towards other men, and
discussions of the nature of man in the learned acad-
emies, have never long remained within the bounds of
private discourse, for what affects the lives of men suffi-
ciently to become a subject of discourse is likely to
become a matter of public interest as soon as social
conditions are favorable. Under such conditions myths
easily replace facts, and myths as a basis for social action can be dangerous.

What men understand to be the nature of man appears to determine their attitudes of conduct towards
men. The conditions and motivations which lead them
to the views they adopt concerning human nature have
only recently become the subject of scientific inquiry
in the more sophisticated English-speaking countries of
the world. Such inquiries are of the first importance
in throwing light upon the origins and reasons for the
views held, and they are most necessary in an area of
human knowledge and action in which prejudice and

pathological thinking have often befouled and be-
clouded the issues and led to the most disastrous social
and biological effects. One has but to be reminded of
the political enthronement of the doctrine of racism
by the Nazis, and of the consequences of this piece of
deliberate political chicanery[1] for millions of human
beings and for civilization as a whole. The white Na-
tionalist policies of the Malan government in South
Africa constitute yet another example of the consequences of pathological thinking on the nature of man.
Pathological thoughts, it should never be forgotten,
can be quite as lethal as pathological germs. Hence,
the importance for human beings of understanding the
true facts concerning the nature of man cannot be
overestimated.

In this little book we shall be concerned with the
critical discussion and exposition of some of the main
problems and findings relating to the biosocial nature
of man, and much of our discussion will be concen-
trated upon a critical examination of the ideas of representative thinkers and workers in this field, those
who have had or may have some influence upon the
thought and conduct of their contemporaries and of
later generations.

The purpose of the present study is not so much
to assess the extent to which human behavior is biologically or socially determined—for no one is in a position to do quite that—as to consider the evidence
which may lead us to a better understanding of the
problems involved. We shall learn quite as much from
the errors of thought and of method which have been
so prominently associated with this kind of inquiry as
we shall learn from such truths as have been established

in relation to it. That the nonscientist should hold many inconsistent and erroneous views in this area of human experience is not at all astonishing. It is an area in which prejudice and emotion have played a dominant role; and scientists have not infrequently revealed themselves quite as prejudiced and emotional, however unconscious they may have been of the fact— as the nonscientist. Thus, it has been shown that scientists who tend towards conservatism in their political views are usually strong hereditarians, misunderstanding the very nature of heredity, and placing most emphasis upon biological endowment as the supreme factor in influencing human behavior; whereas scientists whose political thinking is of a more liberal nature are more inclined to be environmentalists and to give explanations of human behavior mostly in terms of environmental or cultural influences.[2] Similar significant correlations have been discovered in college students,[3] and it is a matter of common observation that the relationship is to be encountered in most classes of human beings. It therefore behooves all of us to keep an open and critically balanced mind in approaching the controversial subject of man's biosocial nature. Absolute certainty is only for uneducated minds and fanatics. Let us, then, in a spirit of inquiry turn to a consideration of some representative theories, from the earliest times to the present day, which have been held concerning the nature of man and which have played an important role in the development of Western civilization, and also to consider some of those which could do so were they to be uncritically accepted.

SPECULATIONS CONCERNING EARLY VIEWS

What is man? What is human nature? These are questions which have undoubtedly exercised the speculative faculty of human beings ever since they became capable of self-reflection. Concerning prehistoric man's reflections upon this subject we know little more than we are able to reconstruct from his cultural remains. From the burial practices of Neanderthal man, who lived some 50,000 years ago, we may infer that he had already developed a thoroughgoing creation story. Man was a creation of the gods and at death he passed on to some other habitation. This is what the tools, the food, and the red ochre found together with the burials suggests. But beyond that, for the prehistoric period, we cannot go. The next best thing we can do is to examine the cultures of living nonliterate peoples, and when we do so we find that the answers to the questions What is man? What is human nature? are usually interrelated in a special way. We find that the answer to the first question is usually returned in terms of what man's nature is culturally allowed to be.

In short, upon investigation we find that most cultures begin with a conception of human nature and

then proceed to fashion their man according to it.
Man is custom made, tailored according to the pattern prevailing in each culture. And as anthropologists
have shown, man's cultures are remarkably various.
Within the great range of human cultures the views
held concerning the nature of man are probably as
numerous as the leaves in Vallombrosa. In point of
fact we know much less than we ought of the views
concerning the nature of man held by nonliterate
peoples.[4] But we do know something, and together
with what we have learned of the views of man held
by the literate cultures of the world, we can say that
these well-nigh exhaust the envisageable possibilities.
A comparative study of the "man-views," as they may
be called, has never been made. It would be most
revealing. The nearest thing to it that we have at the
present time are the studies in culture and personality
that anthropologists have initiated in recent years.
Such studies, in which the attention is largely focused
on child-rearing practices and their relation to the
development of personality, throw considerable light
upon the "man-views" of different cultures, and represent at least one means available to us of discovering
the nature of those views and possibly also those held
by earlier peoples.[5] But beyond the little we have
already said on this subject it is not possible to venture
here. A few words require to be said on biosocial
theories of man in antiquity.

THEORIES IN ANTIQUITY

The ancient Greeks were monogenists, that is to say they believed in the descent of all human beings from a common stock.[6] Differences between men, they believed, were largely due to environment. When, in the fourth century, the institution of slavery began increasingly to come under attack it fell to the lot of Aristotle to develop the necessary theoretical bases upon which to erect the justification for its existence. In the *Politics* Aristotle argued that the slave was but a partial man, lacking the governing element of the soul, and therefore needed to be ruled by those possessing this element. Some men were more fitted by nature to be slaves than others.[7]

Before Aristotle, Plato had deliberately proposed a piece of disingenuous fiction concerning the innate differences existing between men, calculated to convince the workers that there are people who are better qualified to rule than they.[8] But this "Phoenician Lie," as Plato called it, failed to germinate.[9] Most serious scholars are agreed that, with the exception of the lone Aristotle, while the Greeks affected to despise the barbarian, they did so on purely cultural grounds, never

on biological ones.[10] The Greeks, indeed, as Isocrates
(436-338 B.C.) put it, thought of Hellenism as a thing of
the spirit rather than of "race." "So far" he wrote, "has
Athens distanced the rest of mankind in thought and
in speech that her pupils have become the teachers
of the rest of the world; and she has brought it about
that the name of 'Hellenes' is applied rather to those
who share our culture than to those who share a common blood."[11]

What a people thinks of the biosocial nature of man
is reflected, in high relief as it were, in their views on
"race." The Greeks, as also the Romans, were singularly
free of anything resembling race prejudice.[12]

THE CHRISTIAN VIEW

The Christian view of the biosocial nature of man has, it hardly need be said, had the most pervasively influential effect upon Western man's conception of human nature. The Christian tradition has its roots in Greek and Hebrew teachings, from the former deriving its pessimism and from the latter the belief in the innate naughtiness of human nature. The Hebrew-Greek-Christian tradition has been transmitted to us principally through the interpretation given to the teachings of Jesus by a member of the same culture-world. This member was that obsessively uncompromising zealot Saul, called St. Paul. It is to St. Paul that the Western world is indebted for the peculiar development of the doctrine of Original Sin and the inherent wickedness of man—a dogma, so far as we know, not even remotely suggested by anything Jesus ever said or did. With the sinning of the first man "sin entered into the world" according to St. Paul (Romans 5:12-21). St. Paul's teachings were systematically elaborated by the Church Fathers, so that they became accepted doctrine throughout the length and breadth of Christendom. Jansenism and Puritanism are two, by no means

17

extreme, forms of this doctrine, the one holding that
man becomes progressively more evil as he lives, and
the other that the proof of man's inherent evil lies
in his apparently unlimited capacity for enjoyment.
For Jonathan Edwards (1703-1758), for example,

> *In Adam's fall*
> *We sinned all,*

and from the consequences of this sin there was no
escape except by virtue of divine grace.[13] Hannah More
(1745-1833), the English bluestocking, praises the dictum that children should be taught they are "naturally
depraved creatures," and goes on to add that a stroll in
the public gardens on Sunday evening or attendance
at a sacred concert are to be condemned as sinful.[14]

As Muller has remarked: "Throughout Christian
history the conviction that man's birthright is sin has
encouraged an unrealistic acceptance of remediable
social evils, or even a callousness about human suffering. It helps to explain the easy acceptance of slavery
and serfdom, and a record of religious atrocity un-
matched by any other high religion."[15]

To explain the existence of evil the common appeal
of many peoples has been to a "fall" from a prior state
of perfection. Nothing could be more natural than such
an explanation. It is found in early Chaldean legends.
Hesiod (*Work and Days,* 109-201) tells how "the golden
race . . . as gods were wont to live." Then Pandora
ensnared her husband Epimetheus, in disobedience of
the divine command, to open the box with which she
had been presented by the gods, whereupon trouble
and sorrow escaped into the world, leaving only hope
behind.

The early and widespread belief in "the fall," in doctrines of inherent natural depravity, or the original sinfulness of human nature, have enjoyed so wide an appeal, we may suspect, because they have served to shift the blame for man's evil behavior from himself to his inherent nature. He can strive to be good, but always in resistance to the dangerous undertow of his evil and destructive impulses, which are constantly threatening to pull him under.

The secular experience of humanity during the last 2,000 years—the internecine wars, the bloodshed, plunder, treachery and tyranny, the inhumanity of man to man—has in almost every way served to confirm the Church Fathers' view of the natural depravity of man.

The "nasty brute" view of man was developed by Thomas Hobbes (1588-1679) in his book *Leviathan* (1651), and it stated the extreme rationalist viewpoint with force and vigor. Man, argued Hobbes, is simply the motions of the organism, being by nature a selfish, individualistic animal at constant war with all men. Hobbes' influence should not be underestimated.

There is a brief interlude in the long history of the doctrine of man's inner depravity—the Enlightenment or the Age of Reason of the eighteenth century. Adopting a rationalistic and scientific approach to the problems presented by the religious, political, social, and economic issues of the time, and influenced by early explorers' descriptions of "the noble savage," the age tended to take a much more charitable view of human nature.[16] The writings of Kant, Goethe, Lessing, Herder, Rousseau, Condorcet, Diderot, to mention but a few of the most famous, strongly urged the notion of a human nature uncorrupted by any form of original

sin other than the original sins committed against it
by society. This viewpoint was most notably developed
by Rousseau in his great book *The Social Contract,*
published in 1762.

Unfortunately for the Romantics, as they were called
by their more "realistic" critics, the Industrial Revolution interrupted the expansion of their theories. Since
the philosophy of the Industrial Revolution in practice subscribed to the doctrine of the inequality of
man and thus the lesser worth of some human beings
as compared with others, the nineteenth century produced the worst possible climate for the development of
such beliefs as those held by the Romantics.[17] The doctrine of innate depravity was much more suited to the
world outlook of the nineteenth century than was that
of the innate goodness of man. St. Paul, rather than
Jesus, had conquered the Western world.

THE INSTITUTION OF SLAVERY

The French Revolution may not have succeeded in establishing the principle in the minds of men that liberty, fraternity, and equality is sound doctrine by which to live, but it did at least raise the question in the minds of many who would not otherwise have considered it. The history of the last 170 years could, in fact, be illuminatingly written in terms of the clash between those who have attempted to implement this doctrine as a way of life, and those who have attempted to tear it down. It is one of the strange twists of history that the land in which the greatest antagonism to that doctrine should have appeared is the United States of America. As a doctrine to which to pay lip service the principles of the French Revolution were acceptable enough, but when it came to the question of putting them into practice, the 30 per cent profit on each slave stood in the way. When, towards the end of the eighteenth century, voices began to make themselves heard in protest against the inhuman traffic in slaves, and when those voices came increasingly from influential men and organizations, the supporters of slavery, put on the defensive, were forced to look about them for reasons of a new kind to controvert the dangerous arguments of their opponents. The abolitionists argued that those who were enslaved were as good human beings as those who had enslaved them. To this, by way of reply, the champions of slavery could only attempt to show that the slaves were certainly not as good as their masters. And in this highly charged emotional atmosphere there began the doleful recital of the catalogue of differences which were alleged to prove the inferiority of the slave to his master.[18]

It is not commonly realized how greatly so many of the biosocial theories of the nature of man were influenced by the debates which raged over slavery during the period 1775-1870. One side claimed that there were groups of men characterized by physical *and* mental differences who stood lower in the scale of development than other groups; it was also claimed that such differences characterized the different classes of men living in the same society or nation. The other side claimed that apart from the physical differences, so far as the races of mankind were concerned, the mental differences which existed between groups of mankind were probably due to differences in opportunity for mental development, and that so far as class differences are concerned, mental and even physical differences could be traced to differences in socio-economic conditions and opportunities for education. The debate still goes on. It received a new accretion of strength with the advent of the Darwinian theory of evolution, in the age of the Industrial Revolution, associated with a galloping imperialism and the rising tide of nationalism. It is at this juncture that we may profitably turn to a consideration of the various biosocial theories of the nature of man.

THE DARWINIAN THEORY OF EVOLUTION

Darwin's epoch-making book was published on November 24, 1859, and was entitled *On the Origin of Species by Means of Natural Selection, or the Preservation of Favoured Races in the Struggle for Life*. Here, at once, in the very title of this famous book we perceive that it was taken for granted that some races will be favored in the struggle for existence while others will not. Those who have the necessary adaptive fitness will survive, those who do not will tend to leave a smaller progeny behind them and even die out.

We know how well this doctrine fitted the book of laissez-faire capitalism. Here, full-blown, was the scientific validation of the class structure of society, and the imperialist, exploitative enterprises of such a society.[19]

It was not, in fact, till 1871, when Darwin's *The Descent of Man* was published, that what was implicit in *The Origin of Species* was made fully explicit for man. "Man, like every other animal, has no doubt advanced to his present high condition through a struggle for existence consequent on his rapid multiplication; and if he is to advance still higher, it is to be feared that he must remain subject to a severe struggle. Otherwise he would sink into indolence, and the more gifted men would not be more successful in the battle of life than the less gifted. Hence, our natural rate of increase, though leading to many and obvious evils, must not be greatly diminished by any means. There should be open competition for all men." [20]

The implication here is that man is a naturally competitive creature who has attained his present high estate through competition, and if he is to make any progress, he must continue to compete.

This view that man is a naturally aggressive creature, as we have already seen, was by no means the invention of Charles Darwin. Darwin had inherited the notion as a member of the Western Christian tradition, just as Thomas Hobbes, two centuries earlier, had done. What Darwin did was to naturalize, to render scientifically respectable, the idea of "Original Sin"—in its nineteenth-century garb: "innate depravity." Man, in common with the rest of the animal kingdom, he asserted, is naturally aggressive; but though that be the natural fact, yet Darwin adds that "Important as the struggle for existence has been and even still is, yet as far as the highest part of man's nature is concerned there are other agencies more important. For the moral qualities are advanced, either directly or indirectly, much more through the effects of habit, the reasoning powers, instruction, religion, &c., than through natural selection." [21] This is an important statement. It says, in effect, that man's moral qualities are not the product of natural selection, but rather of artificial or social selection, through the agency of what we would today call culture. While man's physical evolution has, in the past, been dependent on natural selection, Darwin tries to show, in *The Descent of Man,* that his moral and social evolution is increasingly dependent upon cultural factors.

It is, however, quite clear from Darwin's standpoint that the allegedly innate aggressive impulses of man are in conflict with his moral strivings. And this is the view which has prevailed up to the present day. Darwin and the Darwinians, in the spirit of their highly competitive times, gave too much attention to competition as a factor of evolution and too little to the factor of cooperation.[22] In *The Origin of Species* there is but a single reference to the factor of cooperation,[23] the emphasis is overwhelmingly upon the competitive nature of living things.

Darwin quite sensitively understood the importance of cooperation for man's future development, but what he failed to observe was that the effects of good habits, reasoning powers, instruction, and religion, etc., insofar as they confer survival benefits upon human beings, had in man's past, and will continue to have in his future, a high natural as well as a high artificial (cultural) selective value. As Haldane has pointed out, "in so far as it makes for the survival of one's descendants and near relations, altruistic behaviour is a kind of Darwinian fitness, and may be expected to spread as a result of natural selection." [24]

The Darwinian view of man's nature became generalized in the following form: Since man is descended from lower animals, and his physical relationship to those animals can be demonstrated by any competent anatomist, it is evident that man carries within his structure the marks of his lowly ancestry. It is, so it was

further reasoned, naturally to be expected that he also
carries within him the evidences of his psychic affinity
to the animals from which he has descended. Competi-
tiveness and aggressiveness are inborn traits of man, so
runs the theory, and they cannot be eradicated; the
problem is to control them.

From Darwin to Freud this is the theme song of innumerable writers, ranging from artists to zoologists,
and embracing military men, emperors, sociologists,
businessmen, politicians, literary critics, musicians, and
the man on the street, not to mention practically every
other class of human being.

Such a "Darwinian" standpoint has been used as a
basis for a wide variety of arguments: for discrimina-
tion against persons on the basis of some group mem-
bership fancied to be "inferior," for the justification
of war, on the conduct of business, or the bringing up
of children. Darwin's statement that "At some future
period, not very distant as measured by centuries, the
civilised races of man will almost certainly exterminate,
and replace, the savage races throughout the world,"[25]
was echoed by innumerable thinkers: Ernst Haeckel in
Germany and the German General Staff,[26] Francis Galton, Karl Pearson, Herbert Spencer, and many others
in England,[27] and most recently Sir Arthur Keith;[28]
by C. B. Davenport, E. M. East, and William McDougall
in the United States,[29] and by numerous others.[30]

Nineteenth-century thinkers had, on the whole, arrived at the conclusion that human nature differs
racially, ethnically, nationally, and even among the
social classes of the same people, and that these differences are biologically determined. Hence, it became a
simple matter to account for the differences in human

nature and their cultural expression. Since the differences in human nature were biologically determined, it became evident that the peoples who had conquered others during the history of the world were superior to those whom they had defeated, and secular world history could be regarded as a continuation of natural history. It has already been pointed out that this conception of human nature gained ascendancy in the nineteenth century with the rise (in the midst of the Industrial Revolution and a rampant imperialism) of the Darwinian theory of evolution and its doctrine of natural selection, the "struggle for existence" and the "survival of the fittest." Intellectually honest men and distinguished scientists could persuade themselves and others that the virtual enslavement of "the lower classes," the exploitation of the lands of "inferior" or "superannuated races" and their eventual supplantation by "the white race," were not only biologically justifiable, but the clear Judgment of Nature.

Galton held that the quality of a civilization was dependent upon the qualities of the individuals composing it, and that the rise and decline of civilizations were associated with the rise and decline of the innate qualities of peoples. Galton took a pessimistic view of man's capacity to maintain civilization at a high level—unless man consciously took into his own hands the matter of securing the persistence of individuals with the highly developed necessary innate qualities. Man, he suggested, could take the breeding of man in hand. For this purpose he proposed a science of "eugenics," which he defined as "the science of improving stock, which is by no means confined to questions of judicious mating but which, especially in the case of man, takes

cognizance of all influences that tend in however re-
mote a degree to give to the more suitable races or
strains of blood a better chance of prevailing speedily
over the less suitable than they otherwise would have
done." [31] Perceive how readily such a view of human
nature leads to the practice of racism and the justification of war. Nowhere is this made more explicit than
in a famous lecture by Karl Pearson, Galton's pupil
and friend, entitled *National Life from the Standpoint
of Science* (1901). Pearson writes, "You will see that
my view—and I think it may be called the scientific
view of a nation—is that of an organized whole, kept
up to a high pitch of internal efficiency by insuring
that its numbers are substantially recruited from the
better stocks, and kept up to a high pitch of external
efficiency by contest, chiefly by way of war with inferior
races, and with equal races by the struggle for trade-
routes and the sources of raw material and of food
supply. This is the natural history view of mankind,
and I do not think you can in its main features subvert
it." (p. 46)

Some twelve years earlier Thomas Henry Huxley
had published what soon came to be known as "The
Struggle for Life Manifesto," in which he asserted that
"From the point of view of the moralist, the animal
world is on about the same level as a gladiator's show.
The creatures are fairly well treated, and set to fight—
whereby the strongest, the swiftest and the cunningest
live to fight another day. The spectator has no need to
turn his thumbs down, as no quarter is given." [32] In
1893, in the Romanes Lecture on "Evolution and Ethics" Huxley made it clear that "the practice of that
which is ethically best—what we call goodness or virtue

how to answer, and therefore we should feel relieved if the whole structure of our arguments were to prove erroneous. The opposition of ego (or death) instincts and sexual (life) instincts would then disappear, and the repetition-compulsion would also lose the significance we have attributed to it." [39]

The problem is again stated in Freud's last (posthumously) published work, *An Outline of Psychoanalysis.* He writes: "If we suppose that living things appeared later than inanimate ones and arose out of them, then the death instinct agrees with the formula that we have stated, to the effect that instincts tend toward a return to an earlier state. We are unable to apply the formula of Eros (the love instinct). That would be to imply that living substance had once been a unity but had subsequently been torn apart and was now tending toward re-union." [40]

In a milieu of war, hostility, divisiveness, destruction, and death, it is perhaps understandable why Freud should have failed to see the answer—which almost any student of biology could have given him—to the question he asked. Freud here presents a striking illustration of the dangers which arise from becoming too enamored with theory, namely, the resulting insensibility to facts.

Of course living substance had once been a unity, and we see this unity at a complex level in the single cell; the "tearing apart" is seen in the process of fission, in the one cell coming into being from the other; and the "tending toward re-union" we see not merely in the conjugal behavior of organisms but in the tendency of organisms to relate to each other, as exhibited in the innate tendency of one organism or cell to react

in a definite manner with another organism or cell—
a process which has been called *prototaxis*.

Organisms are environmental necessities for each
other. The fact that all living organisms tend to form
social aggregates, that is, to interact with each other in
a mutually beneficial manner, is proof of the deep-
seated nature of this universal drive. I have elsewhere
suggested that the fundamentally social nature of all
living things has its origin in the reproductive relationship between genitor and offspring; in the fact that
the life of either one or the other is at some time dependent upon the potential or actual being of the other;
and that the social relationships existing between organisms up to and including man represent the largely
unconscious development of the interdependent relationship between mother and child as experienced in
the reproductive state.[41]

The tendency of life is not to destroy itself but to
reproduce and maintain itself. Sexual conjugation and
reproduction are related not simply as cause and effect,
in that order, but conjugation occurs as an effect of
reproduction. The "repetition compulsion" of which
Freud speaks, the desire to return to the unitary state,
the drive towards union, arises out of the fact that all
living things originate out of other living things. The
drive to be together is an expression of the desire to
be united with one's kind, to be unified without being
reduced to uniformity.

The aim of Eros, according to Freud, is to bind together, whereas the aim of Thanatos is to undo connec-
tions and so to destroy things. "We may suppose that
the final aim of the destructive instinct is to reduce
living things to an inorganic state. For this reason we

also call it the death instinct." [42]

Throughout the writings of Freud the "aggressive instinct" plays an important role. We are told that "The holding back of aggressiveness is in general unhealthy and leads to illness." [43] Freud continually speaks of the "hostile impulses of mankind" [44] as if they were biologically determined and biologically inherited entities; and when he speaks of human culture he says, "one gets the impression that culture is something which was imposed on a resisting majority by a minority that understood how to possess itself of the means of power and coercion." [45] Freud's conception of the cyclopean family, in *Totem and Tabu* (1913), in which the father ruthlessly drives out his own sons; his development of the theory of the Oedipus complex, in which it is postulated that every male child normally develops a profound jealousy of the father's possession of the child's mother; in addition, the concept of narcissism as a stage of self-love in the development of every infant, and many similar notions, were instrumental in conveying a picture of the biosocial nature of man, as an essentially selfish, aggressive creature, driven by blind creative and destructive forces, which it was doubtful that man could ever successfully control. [46]

Freud's view of man's nature has colored much of the thinking of innumerable workers in the social and psychological sciences. Reference may be made to the writings of a contemporary psychoanalyst who belongs to the school of Jung, Dr. M. E. Harding. Dr. Harding writes: "Beneath the decent façade of consciousness with its disciplined, moral order and its good intentions, lurk the crude instinctive forces of life, like monsters of the deep—devouring, begetting, warring endlessly. They are for the most part unseen, yet on their urge and energy life itself depends: without them human beings would be as inert as stones. But were they left to function unchecked, life would lose its meaning, being reduced once more to mere birth and death, as in the teeming world of the primordial swamps. In creating civilization man sought, however unconsciously, to curb these natural forces and to channel some part at least of their energy into forms that would serve a different purpose. For with the coming of consciousness, cultural and psychological values began to compete with the purely biological aims of unconscious functioning." [47]

This is a typical utterance of the Freudian and the Jungian schools of psychoanalysis on the biosocial nature of man. Alfred Adler takes a very different view of man's nature. "The growing, irresistible evolutionary advance of social feeling," he writes, "warrants us in assuming that the existence of humanity is inseparably bound up with 'goodness.' Anything that contradicts this is to be considered as a failure in evolution; it can be traced back to mistakes that have been made . . . to a failure, however produced, in one's growth in social feeling." [48]

Ian Suttie, in what is undoubtedly the most original, profound, and sympathetic of the critiques of Freud, *The Origins of Love and Hate* (1939), finds Freud's view of the biosocial nature of man utterly unacceptable and not in agreement with the facts; he anticipates Adler in showing that the great biologic need of human beings is for sociability and *not* for a combination of destructiveness and love. Karen Horney takes a similar stand in her many books, and so do Erich Fromm and Harry Stack Sullivan.[49]

Freud conceives of man as born with a turmoil of energies, the *id,* which provides the source of the energies out of which the *ego* is, in part, developed, the ego always retaining its roots in the id, and also deriving part of its energy from various organs and parts of the body. But the struggle between *Eros* and *Thanatos,* the binding-together instinct and the death-instinct, is always paramount. "One has to reckon," says Freud, "with the fact that there are present in all men destructive, and therefore anti-social and anti-cultural, tendencies, and that with a great number of people these are strong enough to determine their behavior in human society." Hence, it seems probable to Freud, "every culture must be built up on coercion and instinctual renunciation; it does not even appear certain that without coercion the majority of human individuals would be ready to submit to the labour necessary for acquiring new means of supporting life."[50]

Freud's view of man was a deeply pessimistic one, and this pessimism increased as he grew older. An examination of Freud's own life shows us that he was as much a child of his time as we are inclined to be of ours. Growing up in nineteenth-century Vienna, in a patriarchal family, discriminated against because he was Jewish, struggling for existence in a highly competitive society, Freud early imbibed the compelling Darwinian viewpoint and the conception of man as a brute struggling to be free of his destructive impulses, but increasingly failing in the attempt. That the idea of a death instinct should appeal to such a thinker, even though the conjectures upon which it was based would not bear critical examination, would almost have been predictable in terms of Freud's own life.[51] Psychoanalytic theory, as distinct from psychoanalytic practice, constitutes a reflection of Freud's own acquired nature.

Freud's pessimism is exhibited in a remarkable passage in one of the last of his books, *Civilization and Its Discontents* (1930). Here Freud speaks almost literally in the words of Thomas Hobbes: "Men are not gentle, friendly creatures wishing for love . . . but . . . a powerful measure of desire for aggression has to be reckoned a part of their instinctual endowment. . . . *Homo homini lupus;* who has the courage to dispute it in the face of all the evidence in his own life and in history? This aggressive cruelty usually lies in wait for some provocation, or else it steps into the service of some other purpose, the aim of which might as well have been achieved by milder measures. In circumstances that favour it, when those forces in the mind which ordinarily inhibit it cease to operate, it also manifests itself spontaneously and reveals men as savage beasts to whom the thought of sparing their own kind is alien. Anyone who calls to mind the atrocities of the early migrations, of the invasion by the Huns or by the so-called Mongols under Jenghiz Khan and Tamurlane, or the sack of Jerusalem by the pious crusaders, even indeed the horrors of the last world-war, will have to bow his head humbly before the truth of this view of man."[52]

Freud, tragically enough, was himself to be a victim

of World War II, for it was only with the greatest
difficulty that he was ransomed from the Nazis and
persuaded to leave Vienna for London, where after
some fifteen months he died on September 23, 1939—
the greatest and most influential student of the human
mind who has ever lived.

Freud's pessimistic view of the nature and future of
man has powerfully influenced both psychiatric theory
and practice and all the behavioral sciences. And this
view of man has served, of course, to give the final
validation to the traditional conception of human nature.

What can we do other than humbly bow our heads,
as Freud suggests, to the truth of this so frequently re-
inforced tradition concerning the innate aggressiveness
of man? It may perhaps be suggested that while the
scientific attitude should embrace a certain amount
of humility it is by no means a part of that attitude
to bow one's head even in the face of the so-called
facts, for a fact is at best little more than an interpretation, the consensus of opinion of those who *should*
know. Only too often facts, and even laws of nature,
turn out to be nothing but theories which have been
smuggled across the border without benefit of the
proper customs examination as to their right to enter
the realm of fact. The proper attitude in the face of
facts or theories is not belief or disbelief, but dispas-
sionate inquiry.

Freud expressed the belief of the greater part of
Western tradition when he wrote that "men are not
gentle, friendly creatures wishing for love," but that
they have a "constitutional tendency to aggression

against one another." The question we have to ask, and answer, is: What is the evidence for such statements?

The answer we are given is: The behavior of human beings. Human beings are hostile to one another; they hate, betray, destroy, kill, and murder. The human record, it is alleged, provides a ghastly proof of man's constitutional aggressiveness.

CRITICISM OF THE FREUDIAN VIEW

Let us critically examine Freud's claims for the constitutional aggressiveness of man. It is beyond dispute that the human record provides abundant proof of human aggressiveness. But what that record does not provide is proof of its innateness. And here it may be pointed out that when Freud uses the word "constitutional" he uses it incorrectly, as many others have done before and since, as equivalent to "innate." The fact is that constitution is not a biological *given,* a structural-functional entity predestined by its genotype (the biological endowment of genes) to function in a pre-destined manner, but rather constitution is a *process* and not an unchanging entity, a process in which the organism undergoes development as an expression of the interaction between its genetic endowment and the environment. What is constitutional may be as much what has been acquired by the organism from its environment as what it has acquired from its genetic endowment. Similarly, heredity is not constituted by genetic endowment, but by genetic endowment as developed under the modifying influence of the environment. What the organism inherits is a genetic

endowment *and* an environment, the organism represents the expression of their interactive effects.[53]

The evidence concerning the biosocial nature of
man, as we know it today, does not support the notion
of an aggressive, death, or destructive instinct in man.
In fact, the whole notion of predetermined forms of
behavior in man is outmoded, for man's uniqueness,
among other things, lies in the fact that he is free of
all those predeterminants which condition so much of
the behavior of nonhuman organisms. Non-reflex automatic behavioral responses, except for crying under conditions of distress, the response to the sudden withdrawal
of support, and the response to a sudden loud noise, are
acquired by learning in man, and not inherited by
genotype. The evidence indicates quite clearly that
everything human beings do *as human beings* they
have had to learn from other human beings.

Man is not born with a built-in system of responses
to the environment, as are most other creatures. On
the other hand, man is born with a built-in system of
plastic potentialities which under environmental stimulation are capable of being caused to respond in a
large variety of different ways.

The fallacy committed by Freud and other adherents
of "the innate aggressiveness of man" school is the
simple reductionist or "nothing-but" fallacy, namely,
that man is an animal upon whose animal drives there
has been superimposed (by culture) ways of behaving
which are often in conflict with those animal drives.
The fallacy is to assume that because the biological
heredity of man is transmitted by mechanisms similar
to those operative in other animals and in plants, the
same mechanisms are responsible for fundamental hu-

man behavior. What is true in the purely biological context becomes a dangerous fallacy when it is applied to human material.

The specific human features of the evolutionary pattern of man cannot be ignored. Man is a unique product of evolution in that he, far more than any other creature, has escaped from the bondage of the physical and biological into the integratively higher and more complex social environment. This remarkable development introduces a third dimension in addition to those of the external and internal environments—a dimension which many thinkers tend to neglect when they consider the evolution of man. Nevertheless, there can be no genuine clarity in our understanding of man's biosocial nature until the role of the social factor in the development of the human species is understood.

Man, by virtue of his reasoning abilities, by becoming a "political animal," has achieved a mastery of the world's varying environments that is quite unprecedented in the history of organic evolution. The system of genes which has permitted the development of the specifically human mind has become the foundation and the paramount influence in all subsequent evolution of the human stock. An animal becomes adapted to its environment by evolving certain genetically determined physical and behavioral traits; the adaptation of man consists chiefly in developing his inventiveness, a quality to which his physical heredity predisposes him and which his social heredity provides him with the means of realizing. To the degree to which this is so, man is unique. To repeat, so far as his physical responses to the world are concerned, he is almost wholly

emancipated from dependence upon inherited biological dispositions, uniquely improving upon the latter
by the process of learning that which his social heredity
(culture) makes available to him. Man possesses much
more efficient means of achieving immediate or long-
term adaptation than any other biological species:
these are learned responses, novel inventions, or im-
provisations.

In general, two types of biological adaptation in
evolution can be distinguished. One is genetic speciali-
zation and genetically controlled fixity of traits. The
second consists in the ability to respond to a given
range of environmental situations by evolving traits
favorable in these particular situations; this presup-
poses genetically controlled plasticity of traits. It is well
known that heredity determines in its possessor not the
presence or absence of certain traits, but, rather, the
responses of the organism to its environment. The responses may be more or less rigidly fixed, so that approximately the same traits develop in all environments
in which life is possible. On the other hand, the responses may differ in different environments. Fixity
or plasticity of a trait is, therefore, genetically controlled.

Having a trait fixed by heredity and hence appearing
in the development of an individual regardless of environmental variations is, in general, of benefit to
organisms whose milieu remains uniform and static
except for rare and freakish deviations. Conversely,
organisms which inhabit changeable environments are
benefited by having their traits plastic and modified by
each recurrent configuration of environmental agents

in a way most favorable for the carrier of the trait in question.

Comparative anatomy and embryology show that a fairly general trend in organic evolution seems to be from environmental dependence toward fixation of the basic features of the bodily structure and function. The appearance of these structural features in the embryonic development of higher organisms is, in general, more nearly autonomous and independent of the environment than in lower forms. The development becomes "buffered" against environmental and genetic shocks. If, however, the mode of life of a species happens to be such that it is, of necessity, exposed to a wide range of environments, it becomes desirable to vary some structures and functions, in accordance with the circumstances that confront an individual or a strain at a given time and place. Genetic structures which permit adaptive plasticity of traits become, then, obviously advantageous for survival and so are fostered by natural selection.

The social environments that human beings have created everywhere are notable not only for their complexity but also for the rapid changes to which immediate adjustment is demanded. Adjustment occurs chiefly in the mental realm and has little or nothing to do with physical traits. In view of the fact that from the very beginning of human evolution the changes in the human environment have been not only rapid but diverse and manifold, genetic fixation of behavioral traits in man would have been decidedly unfavorable for survival of individuals as well as of the species as a whole. Success of the individual in most human so-

cieties has depended and continues to depend upon
his ability rapidly to evolve behavior patterns which
adjust him to the kaleidoscope of the conditions he
encounters. He is best off if he submits to some, com-
promises with some, rebels against others, and escapes
from still other situations. Individuals who display a
relatively greater fixity of response than their fellows
suffer under most forms of human society and tend to
fall by the way. Suppleness, plasticity, and, most important of all, ability to profit by experience and education are required. No other species is comparable to
man in its capacity to acquire new behavior patterns
and discard old ones in consequence of training. Considered socially as well as biologically, man's outstanding capacity is his educability. The survival value of
this capacity is evident.

The genetically controlled plasticity of mental traits
is, biologically speaking, the most typical and uniquely
human characteristic. It is probable that the survival
value of this characteristic in human evolution has
been considerable for a long time, as measured in terms
of human historical scales.

The cultural evidence of early man's handiwork suggests that the essentially human organization of the
mental capacities emerged early in the evolution of
man. The populations of mankind during the greater
part of its existence were very small and, for the most
part, widely separated. The suggestion of Sir Arthur
Keith and of others that since man developed in areas
where the available food was limited man had to learn
to survive by cooperation within the group and aggression without the group,[54] is one of those clever specula-
tions which will not, however, bear examination. In

the first place, the areas in which the remains of fossil men have been found show that the available food, both vegetable and animal, was certainly sufficient to maintain small populations during most of the year. Even in the Ice Ages, when life must have been more difficult, mammals, birds, and fish, were not unabundant. As among the Eskimo, where subsistence to this day presents many great difficulties, the populations are small, and so widely separated that there can, in fact, be little opportunity for extragroup aggression, and if there were such opportunity there would be absolutely no point to aggressive behavior so far as subsistence is concerned.

No, the advantages are all with cooperation, intragroup cooperation first and foremost—as for other forms of cooperation, early men were rarely called upon to exhibit them. The important fact for us to understand is that the only form of cooperation it was possible for early man to practice was intragroup cooperation, and *this* was absolutely necessary both for his own and that of his group's survival. It is out of the question to maintain that during the course of man's evolution a high premium was put upon the development of a capacity for aggression The very opposite seems to be true, that in all societies a high premium is put upon cooperativeness, and the aggressive person is generally regarded with disfavor, whether he be a chief, a military leader, or just an individual general nuisance.

So far as the development, by evolutionary means, of aggressive tendencies in man are concerned, the idea can be thoroughly dismissed. Similarly, anything like an instinct or drive toward aggression can be dispensed with, whether we call it Thanatos or the

Death Instinct, for such drives have not only no adaptive
value but a negative adaptive value, and it is therefore
hardly conceivable that, if at any time they ever existed
—which is more than doubtful—they should have been
preserved. It should be obvious that under any and
all forms of social organization, as David and Snyder
put it, "flexibility or behavioral adjustment to different
situations is likely to have had a selective advantage over
any tendency toward stereotyped reactions. For it is
difficult to conceive of any human social organization
in which plasticity of response, as reflected by ability
to profit from experience (that is, by intelligence) and
by emotional and temperamental resilience, would not
be at a premium and therefore favored by natural
selection. It therefore seems to us highly improbable
that any significant genetic differentiation in respect
to particular response patterns, personality types, tem-
peraments, or intellectual capacities among different
populations or races has occurred in the history of human evolution."[55]

The genetic plasticity of the organism *Homo sapiens*
is such that, within the limits of its genetic endowment,
it is capable of being taught to respond in an extraor-
dinary variety of ways to its environment. This is
not to say that at birth man is born the behaviorally
undifferentiated creature that some have thought, for
already in the mother's womb the fetus is capable of
experiencing and responding to a large variety of different stimuli which may leave a deep impress upon
it.[56] It is now established, for example, that an emo-
tionally disturbed pregnant woman may measurably
affect the behavior of the fetus, to the extent of producing a highly irritable child at birth, who has actu-

ally been described as "a neurotic." [57] How can the mother's emotional states be communicated to the fetus? The fact is that her emotional states as such are incapable of being communicated to the fetus, but that the biochemical changes that her emotional states constitute are capable of being transmitted to the fetus across the placenta. The widely prevalent belief that there is no connection between the nervous system of the mother and that of the fetus is based on an out-moded and inadequate understanding of the nature of nervous activity. Nervous changes in the mother may affect the fetus by a simple route, namely, the neuro-humoral system, that is to say, the system comprising the interacting nervous and endocrine systems acting through the fluid medium of the blood (and its oxygen and carbon dioxide contents). The common endocrine pool of the mother and fetus forms a neuro-humoral bond between them. The endocrine systems of mother and fetus complement each other.

All this is not to say that there is anything at all in the old wives' tales of "maternal impressions." The mother's "impressions," her psychological states as such, cannot be transmitted to the fetus. What are trans-mitted are the gross chemical changes which occur in the mother and, so far as we know at the present time, nothing more.

Factors which will influence the fetus *in utero* may be listed as follows: (1) physical agents, (2) nutritional effects, (3) drugs, (4) infections, (5) maternal dysfunc-tion, (6) maternal sensitization, (7) maternal age, and (8) maternal parity (number of previous pregnancies of mother).

We now have some evidence that a fetus can learn

in utero. Fetuses *in utero* will respond to loud noises, to vibration, differences in pitch and in tone. Using this knowledge Dr. D. K. Spelt showed that a fetus at eight months is capable of being conditioned to the sign of an original stimulus. A woman in the eighth month of pregnancy was the subject of the experiment. An ordinary doorbell with the gong removed, so that the vibration was almost silent, was placed against her abdomen several times for five seconds. There was no response at all from the fetus. Then the bell was applied at the same time as the noise was made that induced a jumping response. This was done over and over again, each time pairing the silent vibration with the loud sound. After fifteen or twenty times, the fetus became conditioned to respond to the vibration alone, in the absence of the sound.

We now know that there is more than a modicum of truth in Samuel Taylor Coleridge's remark, made more than a century and a half ago, "Yes, the history of man for the nine months preceding his birth, would, probably, be far more interesting, and contain events of greater moment, than all the threescore and ten years that follow it."

In short, the point we wish to make here is that even if some children did exhibit the evidences of aggressive behavior at birth, or even at some much later period, in the (unlikely) absence of any environmental conditions which might explain it, we should always have to reckon with the history of the individual while he was in the womb.

THE BASIC NEEDS

At birth the child is equipped with an organization of basic needs. Basic needs are those needs which must be satisfied if the organism is to survive; they are: oxygen hunger, thirst, sleep, rest, activity, bowel and bladder elimination, avoidance of pain, and flight from dangerous situations. Sex is not a basic need because the survival of the individual does not depend upon its satisfaction, nor, indeed, does his health. Furthermore, sex does not require periodic satisfaction as do the basic needs; sex may most appropriately be regarded as a biological drive the expression of which is much influenced if not entirely determined by cultural factors.[58]

Satisfaction of the basic needs will enable the organism to survive. But survival is a means to an end, it is not an end in itself. It would seem that the function of life is living; the organism that does not enjoy life hardly considers life worth living. What the organism wants is to live a healthy, enjoyable life. It wants to be loved, and it wants to love. When the human organism is not adequately loved, even though all its physical needs are adequately satisfied, it fails to develop as a harmonic, integrated, happy, healthy human being. The most important nourishment which the infant and the child requires during its development is the feeling that is communicated to it that it is loved, that there is *a* person or persons who loves it, that is to say who communicates to it the feeling that another person is profoundly interested in its welfare, who is there to support and encourage it in its development, to offer it all the assistances and stimulations it requires. The communication of the feeling that you will never commit that worst of all treasons that one human being can commit against another, namely, that you will never let him down, that you will always be there to support him in his need, and that you recognize that his need is to be needed as well as to need. This is love.[59]

It is now known that children lacking such experience of love tend, usually, to grow up as "affectionless characters," suffering from affect-hunger, exhibiting the effects of the privation of love which they have suffered in their own inability to love.[60] Such individuals tend to be overly aggressive. They are problem children and often problem adults—though their problems may assume a number of socially sanctioned forms. Not having learned to love by having been adequately loved, they tend to be exceedingly awkward as social human beings and extremely dependent upon others for love. The social consequences of the presence of such persons in Western societies are serious, contributing largely to the ranks of juvenile delinquents, criminals, and those multifarious seekers after the substitutes for love who, in their quest for power, frequently come to occupy positions of importance and influence and who, often, in the course of arriving at such positions, and in oc-

53

cupying them, manage to accomplish much social and
personal damage.[61]

The evidence is today overwhelming that in order to
become an adequate, healthy, cooperative, loving human being it is necessary to be loved. No child is born
hostile or aggressive. It becomes so only when its desires
to be loved and to love are frustrated, that is, when
its expected satisfactions are thwarted—and the thwarting of an expected satisfaction is the definition of frustration.

THE ORIGIN OF AGGRESSIVENESS

This is what Freud failed to perceive. What he took to be inborn hostility is, in fact, an acquired form of behavior following upon the frustration of the organism's expected satisfactions. Hostility, aggressiveness, and "bad" behavior are simply techniques for securing love, for compelling the attention of those who have refused it. While the psychophysical mechanism to develop aggressiveness as a result of the thwarting of expected satisfactions is inherited, aggressiveness as such is not inherited. The recent students of infant and child behavior are, for the most part, unanimous in agreeing that children are not born aggressive. Thus, Professor Lauretta Bender, the child psychiatrist, writes that hostility, far from being inborn, "is a symptom complex resulting from deprivations which are caused by developmental discrepancies in the total personality structure such that the constructive patterned drives for action in the child find inadequate means of satisfaction and result in amplification or disorganization of the drives into hostile or destructive aggression." "The child" she writes, "acts as though there were an inherent awareness of his needs and there is thus the expectation of having them met. A failure in this regard is a deprivation and leads to frustration and a reactive aggressive response." [62]

Indeed, the developmental directiveness of the organism is towards maturation in terms of cooperation. Bender calls it "the inherent capacity or drive for normality." And she says, "The emphasis on the inborn or instinctive features of hostility, aggression, death wishes, and the negative emotional experiences represents a one-sided approach which has led our students of child psychology astray."

In an important study Professor A. H. Maslow has examined the viewpoint that "man's deepest impulses are bad, evil, undesirable, selfish, criminal, or otherwise reprehensible," and has found it completely wanting. Professor Maslow writes: "I find children, up to the time they are spoiled and flattened out by the culture, nicer, better, more attractive human beings than their elders, even though they are of course more 'primitive' than their elders. The 'taming and transforming' that they undergo seems to hurt rather than help. It was not for nothing that a famous psychologist once defined adults as 'deteriorated children.'" [63]

Professor Maslow puts this viewpoint neatly: "Those human impulses," he writes, "which have seemed throughout our history to be deepest, to be most instinctive and unchangeable, to be most widely spread throughout mankind, *i.e.*, the impulse to hate, to be jealous, to be hostile, to be greedy, to be egoistic and selfish are now being discovered more and more clearly to be acquired and *not* instinctive. They are almost certainly neurotic and sick reactions to bad situations, more specifically to frustrations of our truly basic and instinct-like needs and impulses." [64]

This, essentially, represents the viewpoint of such psychoanalysts as Karen Horney, Erich Fromm, Harry Stack Sullivan, Ives Hendrick, and many others.[65] It is a very different viewpoint from that represented by Freud.

Is there any evidence whatever for the existence of a basic need for aggression? Is there such a thing as an aggressive drive? Has anyone ever observed "aggressive instincts," as Freud calls them, in human beings or the "love of aggression in individuals" as an expression of an "innate tendency to aggression"? I know of no one who has done so. On the other hand, the evidence indicates that the "tendency to aggression" and the "love of aggression," of which Freud and others speak, is not observable at any time in any human being who has not secondarily acquired it.

A distinguished psychiatrist, Karl Menninger, has poured scorn upon "sociologists, anthropologists, and others whose psychological groundwork is relatively deficient" for regarding aggressiveness as "the result of 'the culture' in which the individual lives. They make," he writes, "such nonsensical propositions as that all aggression is the result of frustration. Anyone who has had his toe stepped on, which is certainly not a frustration, knows how inadequate such a formula is. Furthermore it completely ignores the question of where the aggressive energy comes from which is provoked by the frustration, and this is what the instinct theory attempts to answer." [66]

Though he denies that aggressiveness "is the result of culture" and calls nonsensical the proposition that all aggression is the result of frustration, the fact is that the relation of culture to the determinance of behavioral response could not be better illustrated than by this example of toe-stepping. For when a person living in a so-called primitive culture steps on the toes of another, he is likely to do so with bare feet upon toes that are uncornified or otherwise deformed, and is thus unlikely to hurt or frustrate the other and provoke aggressive behavior. Whereas in a culture in which one wears shoes (and bunions impede the pilgrim's progress), one is likely to hurt and frustrate the person upon whose toe one has stepped—but whether aggressiveness will be elicited or not will depend upon the manner in which the stepped-upon has learned to respond to such frustrations. If we accept the generally accepted definition of a frustration as the thwarting of an expected satisfaction, then it may perhaps be acknowledged that having one's toe stepped on may be experienced as a frustration of the expectation of pursuing the

> . . . *noiseless tenor of one's way*
> *Yet e'en these bones from insult to protect.*

We need go no further than our own culture to observe how the response to frustration is bred into one—and is therefore culturally determined. An ill-bred person may react to having his toe stepped on with aggressive behavior, a well-bred person may react with nonaggressive behavior. But this may reflect no more than a difference in the learned ability to control the expression of aggression. On the other hand, the different responses may actually represent a difference in feeling content—in the one case aggressive feeling being present and in the other not present.

Other things being equal, we can take this difference

in feeling to be an expression of a nervous system which
has been socialized in different ways in connection
with the frequency of frustration and the training in
the kind of responses permitted to them. There can be
very little doubt that different culturalizing mechanisms serve to organize the nervous systems of their
owners in very different ways. The evidence from different cultures of the manner in which response to
frustration is trained is most impressive. Anthropologists have made the accounts of these differences so
widely available[67] that even the much-appealed-to man
on the street knows that the Zuni Indians tend to avoid
every form of aggressive behavior, that the expression
of aggressive behavior is institutionalized among the
Kwakiutl Indians of the Northwest Pacific Coast, that
the Dobuans of the Western Pacific are pathologically
aggressive, and that the Arapesh of New Guinea control
some forms of aggression but not others.

Where does all the aggressive energy come from that
is provoked by frustration? This is usually an easy
question for those to answer who have been influenced
by the complex traditions which have been set out
earlier in these pages. Those who pride themselves on
their knowledge of evolutionary theory and those who
have been influenced by that theory can always appeal
to the idea that man has inherited his fund of aggressiveness from his lower animal ancestors. But *are* lower
animals aggressive? Aggression is the overt expression
of a feeling hostility, and the function of the overt act
is to inflict injury upon the object towards which hostility is felt. Upon occasion, probably all animals will
exhibit such behavior, but the occasion has a cause.
In fact, lower animals are no more innately aggressive

than is man. As in man, their aggressive behavior is the response to some frustration or another. Animals do not prey upon other animals because they feel hostile towards them, even when upon occasion they may appear to "kill for killing's sake," but they do prey upon other animals in order to eat. It produces only confusion to identify predatory behavior with hostile aggressiveness as the Freudians do. In spite of Tennyson, who sang of "Nature red in tooth and claw" and the Darwinians who "proved" it, Nature is not red in tooth and claw, and it is an abysmal piece of nonsense to suggest that in a state of nature animals are in a more or less continuous state of hostility towards one another; that the lower animals are naturally aggressive; that, this being the case, man's apelike ancestors must undoubtedly have been so; and that the source of man's aggressive energies is therefore to be looked for in his lowly animal ancestry.

The Darwinian conception of competition as struggle for existence *against* other animals has assumed the form of a dogma. This dogma is more than highly questionable.[68] Darwin himself attempted to avoid the dogma of "struggle-against" others, but often wrote as if this is what he had in mind. Darwin was quite aware of the dependence of all forms of life upon other life as a factor in survival, and that such terms as "struggle for existence" were being used by him in a metaphoric sense; but, as we all know, metaphors have a way of assuming a life of their own which often serves to take the place of the original idea—hence, the danger of all metaphors. It was a simple step to take from the idea of the "struggle-for-existence," with its origin in Malthus' "disease, famine, and war," [69] to "fight-for-life" and "the-survival-of-the-fittest," and thus to think of "competition" as an essentially combative, violent process in which the most successful aggressor established his right to survive; hence the doctrine of "Might is Right."

It does not detract in the least from the greatness and genius of both Darwin and Freud—as well as of others—to realize that they were both so much impressed by the hostility they saw all about them that they projected this upon nature itself, but *we* do not have to make the same mistake. Man's nearest animal relatives are the gorilla and chimpanzee—they are very distant collateral relatives, indeed, and certainly not in the direct line of man's descent. They are not seen at their best behind a cage in captivity—any more than men are, but in the natural habitat to which they are accustomed they are observed to be the most peaceful of creatures. In the first place they are vegetarian and frugivorous, so that they will not harm as much as a fly. They will never attack any living creature unless they are severely provoked, as, for example, by a strange man whom they have never done the least harm who chooses to shoot at them and members of their family. When, under such conditions, the gorilla attempts to protect his family, he is described as "a ferocious beast." The real ferocious beast is not the gorilla but his unprovoked attacker—the more ferocious and the more beastly in a much more profound sense than any beast ever is, because man attacks such creatures in cold blood.

The fact is that man, unable to face it in himself, has projected his own ferocity and beastliness upon the "lower animals," who it then becomes permissible to kill because they are both beastly and ferocious. What

tive or injurious; they may be considered as instrumental rather than goal response aggression. That
is, they are intended simply to aid in achieving grati-
fication of some other drive; they are not satisfying in
and of themselves. Much of the *interpersonal* aggression
observed between the ages of two and four is of this
character, and the true *goal response aggression* becomes noticeable, in many children, only gradually
during that period."[75]

It is absurd to regard as aggressive or destructive
behavior the taking of clocks apart, the removal of the
wings and legs of insects, the breaking and tearing of
objects, and the other seemingly "destructive" acts in
which almost every child has engaged. Observing how
things work represents the expression of an extremely
important stage in the development of the human being, one of whose most powerful urges is the much to
be encouraged trait of curiosity. The best interests of
that trait are not served by treating it as a form of
aggression.

The evidence indicates that all personal aggression,
whether it be of the early nonhostile variety or of the
later hostile kind, is almost always the response to love
frustrated and the expression of a claim upon others to
provide that love. The most extreme forms of destructive aggression, as in murder, are in effect declarations
of the position into which the murderer has been forced
and caused, as it were, to say: If you will not love me,
then I will not love you. Almost always when we witness
aggressive behavior we are observing a demand for
love. This is certainly the meaning of the aggressive
behavior of those small infants who exhibit it—and
it is equally true at all ages.

Thus understood, aggression is not best met with counter-aggression, but rather with love—for aggression is the expression of the need for love, when that love has been unfulfilled.

It is not human nature but human nurture that is the cause of human aggression. Human nature, there is every reason to believe, is good, and treated as such leads to goodness. It is necessary that we understand, in the light of the accumulated evidence, that being born into the human species means that the individual so born is capable of becoming whatever it is within the capacity of that individual to become. The social experience through which the individual passes will largely determine whether he will become a dominantly aggressive or a dominantly loving person, or someone betwixt and between. But there can be no doubt that the individual's drives are originally directed towards the achievement of love, however deformed the process of achievement may subsequently become. There can equally be little doubt that a person's drives are never oriented in a destructive direction, except in severely disturbed cases, and that such disturbances are produced principally by cultural factors.

INFANT-MATERNAL COOPERATION

The psychobiological benefits which are reciprocally conferred upon each other by mother and child are operative from birth. The three great obstetrical problems, which are the concern of every obstetrician, are at once solved when the newborn is permitted to remain with its mother and is put to nurse at the mother's breast immediately after birth. These problems are the third stage of labor or ejection of the placenta, the arrest of the *postpartum* hemorrhage, and the commencement of the return of the uterus to normal size. The sucking of the newborn at its mother's breast initiates nervous reflexes which at once induce contractions in the maternal uterus; the contractions have the effect of detaching the placenta from the uterine wall and expelling it, and at the same time the contracting musculature serves to close off the torn ends of the blood vessels, while the organ as a whole continues to reduce in size. Such are the physical benefits conferred by the newborn upon the mother when it is left in undisturbed relationship to her. The psychological benefits are equally great for the mother. For the newborn the *postpartum* relationship with the mother is of fundamental importance. The sucking at its mother's breast is not only of physical importance to it, but is of the greatest psychological significance.

After a life in the womb and the rather cataclysmic disturbance which is birth, the newborn is called upon to make a number of substantive readjustments to the world in which it finds itself. It must breathe atmospheric air; it must adjust itself to the inflation of its lungs, the reflex rise and fall of the cupolae of the diaphragm, the pressure of the lungs upon the heart, the temperature changes upon its skin, and so on. What it needs most of all during its first few weeks of life is the reassurance that all will be well, and what better promise of good things to come can it be given than the experience at the mother's breast.

At parturition the mother's breast is actively secreting colostrum, an indispensably necessary lemony-yellowish fluid that contains 8.5 per cent of protein as compared with the 1.5 per cent in mature milk which comes in between the tenth and eleventh days, and that carries an unknown number of factors which confer immunities of various sorts upon the infant and also serve to assist the growth of essential intestinal microorganisms. Colostrum also serves as a laxative. From the chemical and physiological standpoints the breast-fed baby is a very different organism from the artificially fed. From the psychological standpoint breast-feeding is important because the psychosocial interchange between mother and infant cannot be reduplicated in an artificial feeding situation, and hence the child, in particular, loses the benefits of an important series of experiences for his own psychosocial development. Experimentally it has been shown that early weaning (before four months), for example, is associated with the later development of a rather pessimistic personality, whereas later weaning (after four months) is significantly associated with an optimistic personality.[76]

That the biosocial development of human beings is significantly influenced by experiences at the mother's breast is strongly suggested by the fact that breast-fed babies tend to walk and to talk earlier than artificially fed babies—not to mention that the survival rates in general are significantly higher for breast than for artificially fed babies.[77]

It should be clear that our cultural arrangements should minister to the needs of man, rather than require the needs of man to adjust to whatever cultural arrangements we seek to make. The physical arrangements of a hospital should not be permitted to determine the human relationships of the mother and her newborn child. The failure to understand the biological effects of breast-feeding, and the overmechanized conceptions that many persons have developed concerning human relations, should not be permitted to determine whether a baby should be breast-fed or not. The facts should be enough. No one should ever take it upon himself to put asunder what nature hath joined together. From the very outset interrelatedness is the state of the developing embryo and fetus, and that is the state in which the newborn and mother are designed to continue. The abrupt interruption of that state under the misguided influence of "modern ideas" is permanently damaging to both mother and child, and to society.

From the very outset interrelatedness is the state

which confers survival benefits upon the interacting organisms; it is the state of interrelatedness which the organism strives to maintain; and any interference with that state, howsoever it may have come about, constitutes an interference with the healthy development of the organism. The evidence indicates beyond any shadow of doubt that all human beings everywhere are similarly constituted in their desire to love and be loved. There is no evidence whatsoever that human beings are born with any individual or group antagonisms as part of their innate structure. Human nature is fundamentally the same everywhere; it is only its secondary or cultural expression which differs.

HUMAN NATURE

There is a widespread tendency to confuse what is culturally acquired and has become habitual by way of human behavior, that is, *second nature*—as it is often called—with what is taken to be inborn, or what might be called *primary nature*. The term "second nature" constitutes a recognition of the fact that much of human behavior is acquired and is to be distinguished from "primary nature."

The fact is that human nature is the expression of the interaction of three complex systems. These are: (1) the genetic endowment acquired through the germ cells of one's parents, (2) the uterine environment, and (3) the cultural environment.

The Genetic Endowment

The Genetic Endowment consists of the chemical packages known as genes which are transmitted on the chromosomes derived from the ovum and the spermatozoon, from mother and father respectively, which produced the conceptus. Genes are giant self-duplicating protein molecules or catalysts. They are estimated to be between 4 and 50 millicrons in diameter—a millicron

is one-millionth of a millimeter; estimated gene size
is therefore between one 250,000th and one 20,000th of
a millimeter. There are about 1,250 genes on each chro-
mosome; and since the sex cells carry 24 chromosomes,
there are probably some 30,000 genes in a male sex
cell and an equal number in a female sex cell. When
these 30,000 genes from the mother and 30,000 genes
from the father come together in the fertilized ovum
the possible combinations are raised to the 30,000th
power—a figure so stupendous that for all practical pur-
poses it can be said that there is no possible chance
in such a gene-system that any two individuals will ever
be alike (excluding so-called identical twins).

Genes do not determine the development of specific
traits or characteristics. There is no specific gene for
tallness, or hair color, or hair form, or eye color—many
genes participate in contributing to these conditions.
But genes are labile enzymes, that is, chemical packages
which vary chemically under different conditions and
tend to accelerate the chemical reactions of other chemical packages. Genes do not act as such in a vacuum,
but they interact with the environment in which they
occur. It is very important to understand this. Development is the resultant of the interaction between the
inherited pattern of genes, the *genotype,* and the environment in which those genes undergo development.
It is therefore incorrect to speak of heredity as the
genes one has inherited from one's parents (one's genetic endowment) for the simple reason that genes
have no functional characteristics apart from an environment, and because the action of genes is to varying extents influenced by their environment.

The child at birth is not what he is because of his

genetic endowment, but because of the interaction of that endowment with all the complexities of the uterine environment provided by the mother.

The Uterine Environment

The Uterine Environment is one in which the developing human organism spends an average of 265½ days. During this period of time, the uterine organism may be affected in its development by any number of factors, predictable and mostly unpredictable. Reference has already been made to the types of influences which may be involved. Inadequate nutritional intake by the mother will almost certainly affect the growth and development of the unborn child, and influence its subsequent growth and development. The mother's use of drugs during pregnancy, such, for example, as quinine, may produce congenital deafness in her offspring. Morphinism has been reported in newborns whose mothers were morphine addicts. Tobacco smoke circulating in the mother's system in the form of the gases which have been taken up by the blood is known to accelerate the heartbeat of the fetus. All such factors are capable of modifying the expression of the genotype, so that the *phenotype,* that is to say the visible functioning organism, presents itself *not* as an expression of its genetic endowment, but as an expression of the interaction between its genetic endowment and its environment.

The genes respond adjustively and adaptively to the environmental conditions acting upon them. Genes determine not traits or characters but the responses of the developing organism to the environment, and the manner in which the genes will determine such

responses will depend upon the environments in which
they act. With modification of the environment the
action of the genes is modified, and therefore the responses which they make.

The Cultural Environment

The Cultural Environment is just as much a part of
the organism's heredity as is its genetic endowment and
its uterine environment. By *culture* is meant the man-
made part of the environment, the pots, pans, writing,
institutions, and the like. Culture, as the late Sir John
Myres (1869-1955) put it, is what remains of men's
past working on their present, to shape their future.[78]
Culture is not only man's means of adjusting himself
to the environment, it is also the means of adjusting the
environment to himself. Perhaps the shortest definition
of culture is that it is the way of life of a people. It
is what people do about the world in order to make
themselves comfortable in it. Cultural behavior is
learned behavior, and practically everything that human beings know and do as human beings they have
learned from other human beings. The distinguishing
criteria of cultural behavior are that (1) it is invented,
(2) it is transmitted, and (3) it is perpetuated.

All learned behavior, that is cultural behavior, is
acquired during the socialization process. When such
behavior becomes habitual it seems "natural," but it
is, in fact, only secondarily and not originally so. We
all speak our native language as if it were "natural,"
but the fact is that in the absence of cultural influences
we should be speaking no language at all. The poten-
tiality for speech is certainly natural, but the languages
we speak are not natural but culturally acquired traits.

Man is human by virtue of the potentialities which he possesses for being a functioning member of human society. It is the extent to which those potentialities are culturalized in society which turns him into a functioning human being, and the kind of functioning human being he becomes will depend upon the interaction between his genotypically influenced potentialities[79] and the cultural influences to which they have been exposed. The culture into which an individual is born and which acts upon him for any durable period of time constitutes his *social heredity,* his genotype constitutes his *genetic heredity,* and his *uterine environment* his *uterine heredity.* Together these three heredities constitute *the* heredity of the person.

It is largely, however, through culture that man makes the distinctively human environment, and largely has it made for him by other human beings, made upon the basis of a unique set of potentialities which distinguish man from all other creatures. Man is tailored according to the prevailing cultural pattern into which he is born. The principal means by which man is culturalized is a system of symbols which are interposed, as it were, between the receptor and effector systems. This system of symbols is language. Language adds a new dimension to the world of man, so that he can be described, as Cassirer[80] and White[81] have done, as the symbol-using animal . . . the *animal symbolicum.*

In the evolution of man this capacity for symbol usage has played a considerable role both culturally and physically, for symbols have exercised an important influence upon man's breeding habits and upon his artificial selection of his own kind.[82]

By cultural means man has doubled his life expectancy in the last hundred years, he has vastly increased the biological representation of his own species upon the face of the earth and has become its dominant species, and he has effectively increased his means of adapting himself to virtually every conceivable environment. By such means he has made it possible for genotypes to establish themselves, which may not have stood much chance of survival if unassisted by the cultural process. All this has undoubtedly affected the genetic evolution of man. Today, more than ever, man has arrived at the means of the conscious direction of his own future evolution. He will increasingly acquire a profounder knowledge of the means of directing his own evolution. The question is whether he will concurrently achieve the wisdom necessary for its proper direction.

THE CHANGEABILITY OF HUMAN NATURE

Since, as we have seen, man's genetic heredity can be influenced by his environmental heredities, it should be clear that any statement to the effect that "You can't change human nature" is the sheerest folly. If it is true that man is custom made, tailored according to the pattern prevailing in the culture into which he is born and in which he is socialized, then as those patterns change so will human nature.

Consider, for example, the seafaring Scandinavians of the Bronze Age, undoubtedly the ancestors of the modern Scandinavians: how different is the cultural behavior of the modern relatively sedentary Scandinavians from that of their raiding forbears!

The boisterous joy in life of the English of Elizabeth I's period is very different from the attitudes of the English in the reign of Elizabeth II. The lusty libertinism of the Restoration contrasts sharply with the prudery of the Victorian Age. The Englishman's "nature" was different in the sixteenth as compared with that which he exhibited in the seventeenth century. In the centuries preceding the middle half of the nineteenth the English were among the most aggressive and violent peoples on the face of the earth, today they are among the most law-abiding.[83]

With respect to the Germans it would be difficult to do better than cite the comments of an eighteenth-century Scottish traveler, William Guthrie, who wrote: "The Germans are by nature honest, hospitable people, passionately fond of liberty, very little versed in dissimulation and artifice. . . . The Germans are brave, and when led by able generals, particularly Italians, have often performed great deeds."[84]

"When led by able generals, particularly Italians," is a remark which, in the light of recent German-Italian military relations, provides an interesting commentary on the mutability of human nature.

And what shall we say of the differences in cultural behavior of such biologically near kin as the New Mexican sedentary Pueblo and the nomadic Navaho Indians, or the behavior of those inhabitants of Mexican Indian villages which are completely Hispanicized?

What can have happened to the "warlike nature" of the American Indians, who today live at peace with their white and Indian "enemies"?

Compare the great Polynesian maritime peoples with their descendants today in Hawaii and New Zealand. Biologically they are mostly the same people, but so far as the expression of their "nature" is concerned they are virtually completely Westernized.

One of the characteristics of human nature is its changeability under changing conditions. The most characteristic trait of man as man is his ability to make all the necessary changes within himself to meet the demands of a changing environment. There is only one defense against the impact of a new idea, and that is stupidity. But man calls himself *Homo sapiens* for the good reason that he alone is capable of reducing the sap in the sapiens. This trait, plasticity or educability or adaptability, is the one upon which, in the human species as a whole, the greatest demands have been made by natural and social selection. Survival of the human species and its progress has depended upon this ability of human nature to change in adaptation to changing conditions.

What most people take to be human nature is really recognized in the phrase "second nature," a nature which has been acquired in terms of the potentialities for being human in a particular culture. Human nature is a pattern of behavior, and this pattern of behavior is known to be capable of change not only from generation to generation, but within the same person in a single generation.

It is because human nature is so often thought of as an expression of biological endowment, and determined by biological heredity, that culture is mistakenly taken to be an expression of biological endowment. Whereas, in fact, human nature is an expression of the interaction between biological endowment and the environments in which that endowment is conditioned, socialized. In the absence of cultural stimulation the organism *Homo sapiens* simply fails to express any nature at all—apart from the phenomena of purely physical functioning, and even here the organism has to be fed by someone else if it is to survive. The cases of semi-isolated children abundantly testify to this fact.[85]

We arrive at the conclusion, then, that human nature is learned or acquired within the limits of those uniquely human potentialities for being human in a particular culture. It is because no other animal possesses such potentialities that it cannot be taught what human beings are capable of learning—hence, educability is the species character of *Homo sapiens*.

Human nature does not undergo an automatic unfolding under the stimulation of the proper conditions; on the contrary, human nature neither unfolds nor develops, but is taught, and it is learned according to the ability of the organism and the kind of teaching which is offered to it. Ability is itself much modified by sociobiological factors of an external nature, such as socioeconomic status, state of nutrition, health, disease, psychic well-being, and the like. What an organism will learn will depend upon all these factors; the kind of things it learns is determined by the culture or segment thereof in which the organism finds itself, and the nature of the organism will be expressed in terms of the cultural conditioning, the socialization process, which it undergoes in a particular culture. If all human beings were brought up in the same culture they would exhibit a basic personality structure of the same kind; they would speak a common language; and they would be recognizable as belonging to the same culture.

"RACE" OR ETHNIC GROUP DIFFERENCES

The reason why great groups of human beings, the so-called "races," exhibit different expressions of human nature, is not that their basic nature differs but because they exhibit the effects of a different history of cultural experience, which experience usually has a long and unique history behind it.

It is not because of any difference in basic nature that the cultures of the different ethnic groups of man differ so much from one another, but because of the differences in the history of the experience which each group has undergone. While it is possible to make this statement with a high degree of probability, it should, however, be pointed out that it is only a probability statement, for we are by no means certain that some biogenic differences in potentialities do not exist between some, at any rate, of the ethnic groups of mankind. What we can say is that, in spite of all attempts to find such differences, none has been found. As the *Unesco Statement on Race* of 1950 puts it: "It is now generally recognized that intelligence tests do not in themselves enable us to differentiate safely between what is due to innate capacity and what is the result

of environmental influences, training, and education.
Wherever it has been possible to make allowances for
differences in environmental opportunities, the tests
have shown essential similarity in mental characters
among all human groups. In short, given similar degrees of cultural opportunity to realise their potentialities, the average achievement of each ethnic group
is about the same. The scientific investigations of recent years fully support the dictum of Confucius (551-
478 B.C.) 'Men's natures are alike; it is their habits that
carry them far apart.' " [86]

The *Unesco Statement on the Nature of Race and
Race Differences by Physical Anthropologists and Geneticists* of 1952 puts it this way: "Studies within a
single race have shown that both innate capacity and
environmental opportunity determine the results of
tests of intelligence and temperament, though their
relative importance is disputed.

"When intelligence tests, even non-verbal, are made
on a group of non-literate people, their scores are usually lower than those of more civilized people. It has
been recorded that different groups of the same race
occupying similarly high levels of civilization may
yield considerable differences in intelligence tests.
When however, the two groups have been brought up
from childhood in similar environments, the differences are usually very slight. Moreover, there is good
evidence that, given similar opportunities, the average
performance (that is to say, the performance of the
individual who is representative because he is surpassed
by as many as he surpasses), and the variation round
it, do not differ appreciably from one race to another.

"Even those psychologists who claim to have found

the greatest differences in intelligence between groups of different racial origin, and have contended that they are hereditary, always report that some members of the group of inferior performance surpass not merely the lowest ranking member of the superior group, but also the average of its members. In any case, it has never been possible to separate members of two groups on the basis of mental capacity, as they can often be separated on a basis of religion, skin colour, hair form or language. It is possible, though not proved, that some types of innate capacity for intellectual and emotional responses are commoner in one human group than in another, but it is certain that, within a single group, innate capacities vary as much as, if not more than, they do between different groups.

" . . . The normal individual, irrespective of race, is essentially educable. It follows that his intellectual and moral life is largely conditioned by his training and by his physical and social environment.

"It often happens that a national group may appear to be characterized by particular social attributes. The superficial view would be that this is due to race. Scientifically, however, we realize that any common psychological attribute is more likely to be due to a common historical and social background, and that such attributes may obscure the fact that, within different populations consisting of many human types, one will find approximately the same range of temperament and intelligence.

"The scientific material available to us at present does not justify the conclusion that inherited genetic differences are a major factor in producing the differences between the cultures and cultural achievements of different peoples or groups. It does indicate, on the contrary, that a major factor in explaining such differences is the cultural experience which each group has undergone."[87]

Most scientists at the present day would subscribe to these conclusions.[88]

There is not the slightest evidence whatever for the racist viewpoint that there is an indissoluble association or linkage between physical and mental characters, that this association is determined by "race," and that this something called "race" is the prime determiner of all the important traits of body and soul, of character and personality, of human beings and of nations. The racists further allege that this something called "race" is a fixed and unchangeable part of the germ plasm, which is transmitted from generation to generation, and unfolds in each people as a typical expression of personality and culture. Associated with the names of Gobineau, Houston Stewart Chamberlain, Richard Wagner, and Adolf Hitler,[89] not to mention hundreds of other lesser "luminaries," there exists not the slightest evidence in support of the racist viewpoint. Nevertheless, this is a viewpoint which has had a very great influence upon Western civilization. The doctrine of racism was so useful to nineteenth-century European imperialism that it would have been invented had it not already existed.[90]

The doctrine of racism gave, as it were, a biological validation to the activities of the imperialists. From the exploitation of primitive peoples or "inferior races" in "outlandish" parts of the world to the "expropriation" of "superannuated races" in one's own and neighboring territories was but a step, the inevitability of which was foreseen by many writers.[91] Enthroned as a political doctrine by Hitler, the tragically disastrous results of this satanism for the Western world are only too recent and too present to require any further reference here. At the present time, in South Africa, the tradition of racism is being deliberately continued as a political doctrine, a doctrine which can only end in disaster for all.

Clearly, the facts about race as science has revealed them make very little impact. Indeed, recent studies have shown that the problem of racism is fundamentally a problem of socialization, a problem of personality development.[92] As Bettelheim and Janowitz put it, "It seems reasonable to assume that as long as anxiety and insecurity persist as a root of intolerance, the effort to dispel stereotyped thinking or feelings of ethnic hostility by rational propaganda is at best a half-measure. On an individual level only greater personal integration combined with social and economic security seem to offer hope for better inter-ethnic relations." [93]

The problem of race is essentially a problem of human relations, and until we improve the means which lead to good human relations the race problem is likely to continue to plague us.

CONSTITUTIONAL PSYCHOLOGIES

A biologistic interpretation of human nature which has been revived in recent years is that of the constitutionalists. Contemporary constitutional psychology is in the direct line of descent from Lombroso (1836-1909), the Italian criminologist and physician,[94] in that it attempts to show that physical and mental traits are significantly related.

Criminals have a special appeal for constitutionalists because they (the criminals) exhibit what is taken to be an extreme form of human behavior, an antisocial form of behavior which has many categories. Criminals, therefore, lend themselves to constitutional studies in a very special manner, for by their antisocial behavior they are presumed to have differentiated themselves from the rest of the population, and hence, if criminals exhibit any special physical traits which do not characterize the law-abiding population either at all or in any such frequencies, there would here be evidence of the constitutional origins of criminal behavior on the one hand and normal behavior on the other.

As far as personality traits of criminals as compared with noncriminals are concerned, it has been shown by

Schluessler and Cressey, who examined 113 studies calculated to throw some light upon this subject, that this series of studies did not provide a consistent demonstration that criminals differ from noncriminals with reference to any personality traits.[95]

THE LOMBROSIAN SCHOOL

Almost all scientific movements are as much the children of their time as are the scientists through whom they come into being. The Lombrosian school of criminology is a case in point. Lombroso, a physician, grew up in the age of Darwinism and Natural Selection. In Italy the fortification of Darwinism assumed the form of a collection of examples of vestigial structures which could be explained only on the basis that they had been derived from some earlier ancestral form. The Italians also particularly busied themselves with the collection of "atavistic" characters, that is, abnormal characters which were taken to be a reversion to an ancestral condition.[96] When Darwin published the second edition of *The Descent of Man* in 1884, his references to such characters were for the most part supplied him by two Italian workers, Canestrini and Ottolenghi. Interestingly enough, under the influence of Lombroso, these two workers became leading criminologists. It need hardly be said that all three brought a strong biological bias to the study of the criminal. All three were physicians and all were strong supporters of Darwinism. Canestrini and Ottolenghi being actively interested in proving the origin of present from past forms by means of vestigial and "atavistic" structures. Is it any wonder, then, that in such a period and with such interests the school of Lombroso should have devoted itself to the attempt to prove that criminals, as a class, are characterized by a significantly higher proportion of vestigial and "atavistic" characters than is the normal population? Such characters were termed "stigmata of degeneration."

Among the "stigmata of degeneration" listed by Lombroso and his school were such characters as asymmetry of the head and skull, projecting eyebrows and jaws, high-pointed head, low retreating forehead, an unusually large or an unusually small head, a long or narrow head, high palate, large outstanding ears, sparse beard, and so on.

The interesting thing about such so-called "stigmata of degeneration" is that they are all perfectly normal characters distributed throughout the populations with which Lombroso dealt. When Lombroso's student Ferri found that 37 per cent of soldiers and about 10 per cent of prisoners showed the "stigmata of degeneration,"[97] Lombroso attempted to explain this startling discovery away with the suggestion that when the stigmata "are found in honest men and women, we may be dealing with criminal natures who have not yet committed the overt act because the circumstances in which they have lived protected them against temptation."

Thus, Lombroso asserted that individuals exhibiting stigmata will be prone to commit crimes under certain environmental conditions. Since a very large proportion of human beings exhibit one or another of these so-called "stigmata," we may unreservedly agree. But what

Lombroso meant, and always reiterated, was that, in almost all cases, it was not the unfavorable environment which led to the commission of the crime, but the biological predisposition to commit it, externally advertised by the presence of stigmata. Lombroso took the "stigmata" to be marks of biological inferiority, proof of the reversion to more primitive forms of biological organization which, in behavior, was reflected in primitive levels of response. This criminal behavior was inseparably associated with biological inferiority. The biological inferiority was held to be the cause of criminal behavior.

AMERICAN CRIMINALS

Interestingly enough, the most recent investigator of the relation between physical structure, as exhibited by external characters, and crime, Professor E. A. Hooton (1887-1954),[98] arrived at conclusions very similar to those of Lombroso. Hooton was a physical anthropologist who had for many years been interested in the origin and evolution of man, and in the description and analysis of the physical characters of skeletal and living groups. The interest and bias of his studies, like Lombroso's, was always biologistic. Hence, when Hooton's report on 4,212 native white Old American prisoners (i.e., of Old American stock) and 313 native white civilians was published, the carry-over of his extreme biological bias evident in the planning of his investigation and the interpretation of his results was not altogether unexpected.

The errors of method and interpretation committed by Lombroso are all repeated by Hooton, except that Hooton does not specifically define the marks or "stigmata" of biological inferiority, but rather takes them to be any of the characters which are distinctive of the criminal aggregate when compared with the civilian sample. "Thus," he writes, "if we find felons to manifest physical differences from civilians, we are justified in adjudging as undesirable biological characters those which are associated in the organism with antisocial behavior. . . . It is the organic complex which must be estimated inferior or superior on the basis of the type of behavior emanating from such a combination of parts functioning as a unit." [99]

"Whatever the crime may be," Hooton concludes, "it ordinarily arises from a deteriorated organism. . . . You may say that this is tantamount to a declaration that the primary cause of crime is biological inferiority —and that is exactly what I mean." [100]

Hooton goes even further and states, "I deem human biological deterioration to be ultimately responsible not only for crime, but for the evils of war, the oppression of the populace by totalitarian states, and for all the social cataclysms which are rocking the world and under which civilization is tottering." [101]

Now, an analysis of the characters studied by Hooton in the light of the biological standards for what are generally accepted to be "advanced," "indifferent," and "primitive" human characters yields interesting results. By such standards it is found that Hooton's criminal series show only 4 per cent primitive, 15.8 per cent indifferent, and 49.5 per cent advanced characters, more frequently than the noncriminal sample!

By biological standards Hooton's criminal series would, on the whole, appear to be superior to his noncriminal series! Whatever such a finding may mean, the fact is that Hooton did not draw his criminal and noncriminal series from the same local, social, economic, and occupational levels of the population, and furthermore, almost half his check sample was drawn from 146 Nashville firemen—an occupation for which, Hooton observes, "the physical qualifications are rather stringent."

In order to make any biological test of differential behavior, it is necessary that both the criminal series and the check noncriminal series be in every respect similar except in the one condition of behavior. The two series must be drawn from the same population or populations, from the same areas, and must come from the same social, economic, and occupational levels. When these requirements have been satisfied, and a significantly higher frequency of certain physical characters is found among the criminals than among the noncriminals, it may legitimately be inferred that there is some significant *association* between criminal behavior and the presence of a high frequency of such characters in an individual or in a group. But to infer from this that such characters reflect the cause of criminal behavior is to misunderstand the nature of causation.

In his investigation Hooton did not satisfy the requirement of equating the conditions of his two groups in all but those in which they were being compared, and he did fall into the error of taking a statistical association to be a cause.[102]

The fact is that Hooton's work throws no light whatever upon any possible relation between physical characters and criminality.

CRIMINALITY IN TWINS

Twins are of two kinds, those deriving from one egg and those deriving from two separate eggs. In the former case they are genetically alike, in the latter they are genetically unlike. If genetic endowment has anything to do with behavior, one-egg twins should be very much alike in behavior, at least significantly more so than two-egg twins. Several investigators have in recent years studied the concordance of criminal behavior in one-egg twins as compared with two-egg twins. When both members of a twin pair were found to be similar with respect to the commission of one or more crimes, they were termed "concordant"; when dissimilar, that is, when one was found to have committed a crime and the other not, they were termed "discordant." In the table below is summarized the findings of one American and four European investigators of such adult twins.[103]

From this table it will be seen that of 104 pairs of one-egg twins examined, 70 were concordant and 34 were discordant. The concordant were almost exactly twice as numerous as the discordant pairs. On the other hand, the two-egg twins showed a discordance almost

CRIMINAL BEHAVIOR OF TWINS

Author	One-Egg Twins		Two-Egg Twins	
	Con-cordant	Dis-cordant	Con-cordant	Dis-cordant
Lange (1929)	10	3	2	15
Legras (1932)	4	0	0	5
Kranz (1936)	20	12	23	20
Stumpfl (1936)	11	7	7	12
Rosanoff (1934)	25	12	5	23
Total	70	34	37	75
Per Cent	67.3	32.7	33.0	67.0

exactly twice as great as the concordance shown in this group of 112 pairs. These are impressive figures, but what do they mean? Professor H. H. Newman, our leading authority on twinning, believes that these figures prove "beyond question that hereditary factors bulk large among the causes of criminal behavior." [104] This is the opinion of all the investigators mentioned, but as a matter of simple fact such studies do not prove any connection whatever between hereditary factors of a genetic nature and criminal behavior. Of this, Newman, who has perhaps observed more twins than any other scientist, is quite aware, for he writes: "The only serious criticism I have known to be aimed at the twin method of studying the factors of crime is that one-egg twins far more than two-egg twins are close companions in their social activities and are therefore more likely to encounter together such social influences as might lead to criminal behavior. This is one more instance of lack of control features in nature's scientific experiments, for it can hardly be maintained that the social environment of two-egg pairs is as closely similar as that of one-egg pairs. Therefore, environmental similarities may to some extent account for the close concordance in crime of one-egg twins, while lack of any such similarity in environment may to an equal extent account for lack of concordance in crime of two-egg twins. Undoubtedly the study of crime by means of the twin method is less simple than it seemed at the outset." [105]

This is, of course, the crucial point. The factor of environment has been virtually completely omitted from these studies of criminal behavior in twins. Hence, the attribution of the behavior of such twins to genetic factors may be written off as completely unproven.

If the genetic theory of the causation of crime is to be consistent, the proportion of two-egg twins who are both affected should be higher than the proportion of one-egg twins where only one is affected. The actual proportions, however, are almost identical, being 33.0 per cent for two-egg concordance, and 32.7 per cent for one-egg discordance. Furthermore, as Reckless has pointed out, "If biological determination of destiny is correct, a discordant monozygotic [one-egg] twin set should be impossible, whereas discordant dizygotic [two-egg] sets should be frequent." [106] The actual findings, however, reveal that one-third of the one-egg pairs of twins investigated were discordant. Why did not the hereditary factor for crime declare itself in one of the members of this one-third of single-egg twins? If the answer is that an environmental factor was probably operative in these cases, a factor which was absent in the case of the criminal sibling, then the theory of the genetic cause of crime collapses beyond repair; for it then becomes obvious that it was the absence of such environmental factors, or the presence of others, that was the one indispensable condition in the causation of the criminal behavior!

It appears, then, that just as environmental conditions are necessary to organize and produce a human mind, so, too, environmental conditions are necessary to organize genetically determined elements of the nervous system so that they can develop and function, or not, in ways which society terms "criminal." In point of fact there is not the slightest evidence that anyone ever inherits a tendency to commit criminal acts. Crime is a socially produced condition, not a biological one.[107]

THE SOCIAL NATURE OF CRIME

Habitual crime may be regarded as a trade or profession, licitly or illicitly pursued, like any other; a trade or profession which is entered and pursued because, in many cases, it was the only one which was open to those who adopted it—socially open, *not* biologically open. Everyone agrees that there is a high correlation between poverty and crime, although criminals are by no means drawn exclusively from impoverished environments. Poverty itself is rarely a cause cf crime, but in the group of necessary conditions which constitute the cause of crime in any one instance, it is of very frequent occurrence. This in itself would suggest that the larger proportion of crimes are committed by individuals who are making an effort to survive. Taken together with all the evidence—cultural, physical, and biological—it would suggest that crime is an adaptive form of behavior which is, in most cases, resorted to by the individual in order to secure himself against a real or imagined insecurity. From the biological standpoint, therefore, criminal behavior, with relatively few exceptions, represents a more or less successful adaptation to a difficult situation. From the social standpoint, such behavior cannot be regarded as unsuccessful; it can only be regarded as undesirable and socially unallowable. But man is not merely a biological creature, he is a biosocial creature, and the effects of criminal behavior upon him as a biosocial organism are likely to be harmful to him as a person, that is to say as a member of society, and harmful also to his society.

It is in the making of human beings, largely during the socialization process, that criminals are made. Genes and chromosomes almost certainly don't make criminals, but social conditions almost certainly do. Why are Americans so much more addicted to crimes of violence than the English? Is it because of a difference in their genetic structure? Why are the American homicide and alcoholic rates the highest in the world?[108] Is it because Americans differ significantly in their genetic structure from the rest of the so-called civilized peoples of the world, or is it, perhaps, because of the prevalence of certain social conditions in the United States as compared with the conditions prevailing in other lands?[109] There can be very little doubt that the genetic differences existing among members of different nations of European origin are far too small to be held accountable for the national differences in crime and alcoholic rates. There can be no doubt whatever that these differences in national crime and alcoholic rates are due to social causes principally and primarily.

It is society, *not* the individual, that creates the conditions which encourage the development of criminal behavior.[110] Our society is in many ways disorganized and disharmonious.[111] And one of the root reasons for this has been the failure to understand the true nature of man, and to socialize and educate him accordingly.

The disorganization and disharmony are not genetic but social in origin, and to repeat once more, it is not man's biological but his social disharmony and disorganization which largely determine who will and when he will become a committer of crimes.

CONSTITUTION

"Constitution" is one of those portmanteau words into which one can fit almost any meaning one desires—but a word which can mean anything in fact means nothing. Nevertheless, the "nothing" that it means at any particular time may most effectively serve to increase one's ignorance. Mostly the word is taken to mean in common parlance the particular type of body build and mental character of the person plus his genetic predispositions to react to the environment. In other words, it is generally supposed that there is a linkage between one's genetic endowment, body build, and mental character. That there does in fact exist such a relationship, at least to some degree, is certain. It is beyond question that genetic factors exercise a major effect upon the development of body type, however subject to the modifying influences of the environment the development of body type may be. What, however, has not yet been satisfactorily demonstrated is that certain body types are linked with certain behavioral or mental qualities.

Contemporary students of constitution take it to mean the sum total of the structural, functional, and psychological characters of the individual. Constitution, they assume, is in large part genetically determined, but influenced in varying degrees by environmental factors. It is taken to fluctuate in varying degrees over a wide range of normality, occasionally crossing an arbitrary boundary into abnormality or pathology.

The problem in studying constitution is a formidable one: it is no less than the attempt to analyze and define the relations of its component parts in the individual. The ultimate goal of constitutional studies is the development of a constitutional typology which will permit the classification of individuals into constitutional types. This is obviously an extremely difficult problem, and although much work has been done in this field, the study of constitution is still in its very early beginnings, while the relationships it seeks to discover and elucidate are still largely in the realm of unsolved problems.

The most ambitious and most widely known constitutional typology today is that of W. H. Sheldon.

Sheldon recognizes three basic and extreme types of physique. He regards each major or dominant aspect of these types as something which, in different amounts, enters into the making of every normal body. These types are described as *components,* as follows:

1. *The endomorphic* or *first component,* characterized by relative predominance of soft roundness throughout various regions of the body. When endomorphy is dominant, digestive viscera are massive and tend, relatively, to dominate the body economy. The digestive viscera are principally derived from the endoderm (the innermost layer of the primordial embryological layers).

2. *The mesomorphic* or *second component,* characterized by relative predominance of muscle, bone, and connective tissue. The mesomorphic physique is normally heavy, hard and rectangular in outline. Bone and muscle are predominant, and the skin is made thick by heavy underlying connective tissue. The entire body economy is dominated, relatively, by tissues derived from the mesoderm (the middle layer of the primordial embryological layers).

3. *The ectomorphic* or *third component,* characterized by relative predominance of linearity. In proportion to his mass, the ectomorph has the greatest surface area and hence relatively the greatest sensory exposure to the outside world. Relative to his mass, he also has the largest brain and central nervous system. In a sense, therefore, his body economy is relatively dominated by tissues derived from the ectoderm (the outermost of the primordial embryological layers).

Sheldon claims that these morphologic components to some extent are found in every individual, on a sliding scale from very high to very low, and he rates the components from 1 for very low to 7 for very high, with 4 standing for intermediate between 1 and 7. Thus, an extreme endomorph would exhibit the somatotype (as it is called) of 711—very high in endomorphy, and very low in both meso- and ecto-morphy. An extreme mesomorph would be 171, and an extreme ectomorph would be 117.

Sheldon claims to have found high correlations between the somatotypes and temperament.[112] Most other investigators have not been able to corroborate Sheldon's claims.

In one of his later studies Sheldon has reported his

findings on some 200 delinquent youths. The impression which this study makes, it must be frankly acknowledged, is a dismal one. It is difficult to gain an idea as to whether the 200 youths examined represented a random sample of the institutional population in which they were examined, or what, indeed, that population was supposed to be. Sheldon defines delinquency as "disappointingness," and as the great American criminologist Edwin D. Sutherland has suggested in a devastating critique of Sheldon's study, "the feelings of Dr. Sheldon are obviously the criterion of disappointingness."[113] In one of his pages Sheldon tells us that "delinquent performance is failure to use religious energy in such a way as to secure, protect, and guide the biological future of the species."[114] This definition makes most people delinquent, and this is exactly what Sheldon says. He finds that the entire number of criminals in his series, a total of 16, are endomorphic mesomorphs. He states that 16 of the most famous generals in history or vigorously successful businessmen or leading politicians would fall into the same somatotypic classification. To be an endomorphic mesomorph "means energetic vitality and freedom from inhibition, two cardinal factors in success at most of the things men undertake. . . . Two professions which I hope are otherwise unrelated appear especially to call for these qualities. They are professional criminality and the writing of fiction."[115] Sheldon does not suggest that endomorphic mesomorphy "predisposes toward criminality, but it might mean that to make a go of being a criminal requires a certain amount of guts that is usually found only" in this somatotype. This is *precisely* the point. There is a certain amount of social selection at work in criminal as for many other types of social and antisocial activities—clearly, the robust, big-chested, tough-looking male has a great advantage over the roly-poly endomorph, or the long, linear ectomorph, if he is to embark upon a criminal career necessitating the use of some strength and even violence. But Sheldon inclines to attribute this selection more to "guts" than to "occupational requirements"—in this opinion he stands with Hooton, with whom he identifies himself, virtually alone. "Perhaps," he writes, "the persistently criminal boy is expressing not so much a 'psychogenic resentment' against the mother as a Dionysian reaction which is almost as much a product of his constitutional design as the way he walks."[116]

It is quite evident, as one reads Sheldon, that he believes man to be in a state of biological deterioration from which he can be saved only by the necessary eugenic planning, and that unless this is done civilization is doomed. This is the burden of the last section of *Varieties of Delinquent Youth*. In the final analysis human nature and body type are indissolubly correlated, according to Sheldon; hence, if we are to safeguard our civilization against the wrong body-types we ought to have a sort of national registry of body-types, so that we could have them under proper control. "For a fraction of the cost of maintaining the rearguard palliation that we do against cancer, which may be only one kind of hereditary constitutional disease, we could keep central files of standardized photographs of the entire population. Such photographs taken periodically for a half-dozen generations, and accompanied by concise medical and social histories, might accomplish more against remediable ills that beset human life (including cancer) than would even a first-rate semifinal war against Russia."[117]

It would be possible to go on citing numerous examples of Sheldon's infatuation with his method and conclusions, both of which have been described as "the higher and the lower phrenology"; but it must in all fairness be said, in spite of Sheldon's own extremes, that he has substantially helped to illuminate the difficulties inherent in the problem which he set himself to solve. The existence of a relationship between constitution and disease is understandable, but the alleged existence of such a relationship between constitution and behavior is a matter of a totally different sort. Human behavior is on a very different plane of integration from that upon which disease has its being; the latter is largely a function of biological factors, the former chiefly of social learning and experience. Constitutionalists habitually commit the pathetic biologistic error of taking man to be largely a function of his genes, forgetting altogether that all genes undergo expression through the alembic of a complex environment.

It is important to understand that constitution, body-type, and genotype are not the same things. Constitution is the aggregate of characters, structural, functional, and mental of the individual, which are in part determined by genes and in part by environment. Obviously, then, constitution embraces both genetic factors and body-type. The genotype is the total genetic endowment of the individual; body-type is one expression of that genetic endowment in interaction with the environment. It should be clear that useful knowledge of the relationship of constitution to temperament and to disease will require, on the one hand, the tracking down of the possible genes involved and, on the other, the environmental factors in the presence of which they have expressed themselves.

Constitution, it cannot be too often repeated, is not predestination. It is in large measure an integral of genetic potentialities influenced in varying degrees by internal and environmental factors. Since this is so there is nothing ever final with respect to constitution, because, as has already been pointed out, it is not a predetermined unfluctuating or unchangeable entity, but a dynamic process more or less continuously modifiable, within limits, through the action of the environment. And in that fact lies man's best hope for the future, for to whatever extent that statement is true to that extent man can control his heredity through the intelligent use of his environment.

CONCLUSION

We must conclude. Thus far all attempts to establish an integral relationship between traits of the body and behavior have failed. The problem, however, is still in its exploratory stage of development. Success, if it is ever achieved, will undoubtedly prove to be so in a statistical sense, that is to say, that some correlations between traits may be found which will permit prediction only within fairly wide limits.

What we need to understand as students of man is that the biosocial nature of man is such that he may be truly described as the most unique of all living creatures, by virtue of his possession—in so highly developed a degree—of the capacity for learning. Indeed, the species character which should be part of the definition of *Homo sapiens* is educability. Man is the most plastic, the most educable, the most malleable of all the creatures on the face of the earth; the creature beyond all others, which makes ridiculous the reductionist fallacy which has it that man is "nothing but" a function of his genes. In reality, man is the only creature who is capable of controlling the expression of his genes, through the manipulation of the social environment in which they undergo development. Educability is man's most important species trait, overshadowing all others. It, therefore, cannot be too strongly urged that education is the principal means through which we can achieve the realization of man's evolutionary destiny. What that evolutionary destiny is we can already begin dimly to perceive; at the present time it looks very much as if it is to live as though to live and love were one.

TABLES

TABLE 1

HOMICIDE AND SUICIDE RATES PER 100,000 OF ADULT
POPULATION

Country	Homocide	Suicide
United States	8.50	15.52
Italy	7.38	7.67
Finland	6.45	23.35
Spain	2.88	7.71
Portugal	2.79	14.24
Canada	1.67	11.40
Australia	1.57	13.03
France	1.53	14.83
Switzerland	1.42	33.72
Sweden	1.01	19.74
Denmark	0.67	35.09
England & Wales	0.63	13.43
Ireland (Republic)	0.54	3.70
Scotland	0.52	8.06
Norway	0.38	7.71
Northern Ireland	0.13	4.82

Source: Fromm, *The Sane Society*, 1955. Based on *Annual
Epidemiological and Vital Statistics, 1939-46. Part I. Vital
Statistics and Causes of Death* (Geneva: World Health
Organization, 1951). The figures in Table 1 are for the
year 1946.

TABLE 2

ESTIMATED NUMBER OF ALCOHOLICS PER 100,000 OF ADULT
POPULATION

Country	With or without complications	
United States	3,952	(1948)
France	2,850	(1945)
Sweden	2,580	(1946)
Switzerland	2,385	(1947)
Denmark	1,950	(1948)
Norway	1,560	(1947)
Finland	1,430	(1947)
Australia	1,340	(1947)
England & Wales	1,100	(1948)
Italy	500	(1942)

Source: Fromm, *The Sane Society,* 1955. Based on the
Report on the First Session of the Alcoholism Subcom
mittee, of the Expert Committee on Mental Health, (Geneva: World Health Organization, 1951).

NOTES

1 In a conversation with Hermann Rauschning, Hitler said: "I know perfectly well, just as well as all those tremendously clever intellectuals, that in the scientific sense there is no such thing as race. But you, as a farmer and cattle-breeder, cannot get your breeding successfully achieved without the conception of race. And I as a politician need a conception which enables the order which has hitherto existed on historic bases to be abolished and an entirely new and anti-historic order enforced and given an intellectual basis. . . . With the conception of race, National Socialism will carry its revolution abroad and recast the world." Hermann Rauschning. *The Voice of Destruction* (New York: Putnam, 1940), p. 232.

2 A study specifically devoted to this subject is that of Nicholas Pastore, *The Nature-Nurture Controversy* (New York: King's Crown Press, 1949).

3 T. W. Adorno, E. Frenkel-Brunswick, D. J. Levenson, and R. Nevitt Sanford, *The Authoritarian Personality* (New York: Harper & Bros., 1950). For a translation of this technical study into a briefer and more readable form see Selma Hirsh, *The Fears Men Live By* (New York: Harper & Bros., 1955).

4 The nearest approach to such a study is contained in Paul Radin, *Primitive Man as a Philosopher* (New York: Appleton-Century, 1927). See also J. G. Frazer, *Creation and Evolution in Primitive Cosmogenies* (London & New York: Macmillan, 1935).

5 J. J. Honigmann, *Culture and Personality* (New York: Harper & Bros., 1954).

6 E. E. Sikes, *The Anthropology of the Greeks* (London: David Nutt, 1914).

7 Aristotle, *Politics*, Book I, Chapter II. To this Rousseau made the effective reply: "Aristotle said," he writes, "that men were not naturally equal, but that some were born for slavery, and others for domination. Aristotle was right, but he took the effect for the cause.

113

Every man is born in slavery, nothing more certain. Slaves lose all in their chains, even the desire to leave them; they love servitude as the companions of Ulysses loved brutishness. If then, there are slaves by nature, it is because there have been slaves contrary to nature. Force made the first slaves, their cowardice perpetuated them." Rousseau, *The Social Contract,* Book I, Chapter II.

8 Plato, *The Republic,* 547a.

9 R. Eisler, "Metallurgical Anthropology in Hesiod and Plato and the Date of a 'Phoenician Lie,'" *Isis,* Vol. 40 (1949), pp. 108-112. See also Karl R. Popper, *The Open Society and Its Enemies* (Princeton: Princeton University Press, 1950) ; and Ernst Cassirer, *The Myth of the State* (New Haven: Yale University Press, 1946), pp. 61-77.

10 R. Schlaifer, "Greek Theories of Slavery from Homer to Aristotle," *Harvard Studies in Classical Philology,* Vol. 47 (1936), pp. 165-204; F. M. Snowden, Jr., "The Negro in Ancient Greece," *American Anthropologist,* Vol. 50 (1948), pp. 31-44.

11 Isocrates, *Panegyricus,* 4, 50.

12 A. Diller, *Race Mixture Among the Greeks Before Alexander,* "Illinois Studies in Roman Language and Literature" (Urbana: University of Illinois, 1937) ; M. P. Nilsson, "The Race Problem of the Roman Empire," *Hereditas,* Vol. 2 (1921), pp. 370-390; F. G. Detweiler, "The Rise of Modern Race Antagonisms," *American Journal of Sociology,* Vol. 38 (1932), pp. 738-747; M. McClure, "Greek Genius and Race Mixture," *Studies in the History of Ideas,* Vol. 3 (1935), pp. 25-33; T. J. Haarhoff, *Stranger at the Gate* (New York: Macmillan, 1948); S. Davis, *Race Relations in Ancient Egypt* (New York: Philosophical Library, 1951).

13 O. E. Winslow, *Jonathan Edwards* (New York: Macmillan, 1940).

14 H. J. Muller, *The Uses of the Past* (New York: Oxford University Press, 1952), p. 160.

15 G. R. Taylor, *Sex in History* (New York: Vanguard Press, 1954), p. 207.

16 R. B. Mowat, *The Age of Reason* (London: Harrap: 1934); Ernst Cassirer, *The Philosophy of the Enlightenment* (Boston: Beacon Press, 1955); H. N. Fairchild, *The Noble Savage* (New York: Columbia University Press, 1928) ; H. Baker, *The Dignity of Man* (Cambridge: Harvard University Press, 1947).

17 See John and Barbara Hammond, *The Bleak Age* (London: Pelican Books, 1947).

18 M. F. Ashley Montagu, *Man's Most Dangerous Myth: The Fallacy of Race,* 3rd ed. (New York: Harper & Bros., 1952); W. E. Dodd, *The Cotton Kingdom* (New Haven: Yale University Press, 1919) ; J. S. Redding, *They Came in Chains* (Philadelphia: Lippincott, 1950) ; J. H. Franklin, *From Slavery to Freedom* (New York: Knopf, 1947).

19 Karl Marx (1818-1883) so much appreciated Darwin's work that he thought of dedicating *Das Kapital* to him. Reading *The Origin of Species* in 1860, Marx wrote to Engels, "Darwin's book is very important and serves me as basis in natural science for the class struggle in history." *The Correspondence of Marx and Engels* (New York: International Publishers, 1935), pp. 125-126.

20 C. Darwin, *The Descent of Man* (London: John Murray, 1871), Chap. 21.

21 *Ibid.*

22 M. F. Ashley Montagu, *Darwin, Competition, and Cooperation* (New York: Abelard-Schuman, 1952).

23 Thus, in *The Origin of Species* Darwin made this very important statement which both he and his followers proceeded to ignore virtually completely: "I should premise that I use the term Struggle for Existence in a large and metaphorical sense, including dependence of one being upon another, and including (which is more important) not only the life of the individual, but success in leaving progeny. Two canine animals in a time of dearth, may be truly said to struggle with each other which shall get food and live. But a plant on the the edge of a desert is said to struggle for life against the drought, though more properly it should be said to be dependent on the moisture. . . . In these several senses, which pass into each other, I use for convenience sake the general term of struggle for existence." Charles Darwin, *The Origin of Species,* Chap. 3, p. 62.

24 J. B. S. Haldane, *The Causes of Evolution* (New York: Longmans, 1935), p. 131.

25 C. Darwin, *The Descent of Man* (London: John Murray, 1871), Part I, Chap. VI.

26 Ernst Haeckel, *Freedom in Science and Teaching* (New York: Appleton, 1879). In a much later little-known work, Haeckel wrote as follows: "The social laws which the organisms follow in their evolution must be traced through the whole scale of life, down to the lowest forms: and it will become apparent that the social impulses or instincts are already existent in the one-celled protists, and spring from the mutual sympathy of homogenous cells, from the social feelings and needs of elementary organisms of a kind. . . . Out of these have gradually unfolded the social inclinations and combinations of a higher order, such as the herds, communities, and states of higher animals, which finally gave rise to the social laws of human ethics. The great advantages that the individuals composing a society derive from it—mutual aid, protection against danger, assurance of food supply—are the causes why the individual instinct of self-preservation is translated into the altruistic instinct of social preservation." Ernst Haeckel, *Eternity: World-War Thoughts on Life and Death, Religion, and the Theory of Evolution* (New York: Truth Seeker Co., 1916),

pp. 127-128. See also F. von Bernhardi, *Germany and the Next War* (New York: Longmans, 1911).

27 F. Galton, *Hereditary Genius* (London & New York: Macmillan, 1869), and *Inquiries into Human Faculty and its Development* (New York & London: Macmillan, 1883); K. Pearson, *National Life from the Standpoint of Science* (London: Black, 1901), and *The Groundwork of Eugenics* (London: Dulau, 1909); Herbert Spencer, *Principles of Sociology* (New York: Appleton, 1876-1880).

28 A. Keith, *The Place of Prejudice in Modern Civilization* (New York: John Day, 1931), *Essays on Human Evolution* (New York: Putnam, 1947), and *A New Theory of Human Evolution* (New York: Philosophical Library, 1948).

29 C. B. Davenport, *Heredity in Relation to Eugenics* (New York: Holt, 1911); C. B. Davenport and Morris Steggerda, *Race Crossing in Jamaica* (Washington: Carnegie Institution of Washington, 1929); E. M. East, *Mankind at the Crossroads* (New York: Scribner, 1923), and *Heredity and Human Affairs* (New York: Scribner, 1927); W. McDougall, *Is America Safe for Democracy?* (New York: Scribner, 1921), and *Ethics and Some Modern World Problems* (New York: Putnam, 1924).

30 For an excellent general review of the subject see G. Nasmyth, *Social Progress and the Darwinian Theory* (New York: Putnam, 1916). See also R. Hofstadter, *Social Darwinism in American Thought* (Boston: Beacon, 1955).

31 F. Galton, *Inquiries into Human Faculty and Its Development,* 1883.

32 T. H. Huxley, "The Struggle for Existence: A Programme," *Nineteenth Century*, Vol. 23, pp. 161-180.

33 The lecture is reprinted in the excellent book edited by Julian Huxley, *Touchstone for Ethics* (New York: Harper & Bros., 1947). The quotation above is from pp. 91-92.

34 *Ibid.,* p. 234.

35 Arthur Keith, *The Place of Prejudice in Modern Civilization* (New York: John Day, 1931).

36 *Ibid.,* and Arthur Keith, *Essays on Human Evolution* (New York: Putnam, 1947), and *A New Theory of Human Evolution* (New York: Philosophical Library, 1948). See also his *An Autobiography* (New York: Philosophical Library, 1950).

37 S. Freud, *Beyond the Pleasure Principle* (London: Hogarth Press, 1922), p. 26.

38 S. Freud, *An Outline of Psychoanalysis* (New York: Norton, 1949), p. 20.

39 S. Freud, *Beyond the Pleasure Principle,* p. 55.

40 S. Freud, *An Outline of Psychoanalysis,* p. 20

[41] M. F. Ashley Montagu, *The Direction of Human Development* (New York: Harper & Bros.,1955), and *On Being Human* (New York: Abelard-Schuman, 1950).

[42] S. Freud, *An Outline of Psychoanalysis*, p. 20.

[43] *Ibid.*, p. 22.

[44], [45] S. Freud, *The Future of an Illusion* (London: Hogarth Press, 1928), p. 10.

[46] S. Freud, *Beyond the Pleasure Principle* (1922), and *Civilization and Its Discontents* (1930).

[47] W. E. Harding, *Psychic Energy* (New York: Pantheon Books, 1947), p. 1.

[48] Alfred Adler, *Social Interest: A Challenge to Mankind* (New York: Putnam, 1938), p. 48.

[49] For an excellent account of the theories of the representative schools of psychoanalysis see Patrick Mullahy, *Oedipus Myth and Complex* (New York: Grove Press, 1955). For a critique of the Freudian revisionists see Herbert Marcuse, *Eros and Civilization* (Boston: Beacon Press, 1955).

[50] S. Freud, *The Future of an Illusion* (London: Hogarth Press, 1928), p. 11.

[51] See Ian Suttie's brilliant analysis of Freud and psychoanalytic theory in such terms in his chapter "Freudian Theory Is Itself a Disease," in *The Origins of Love and Hate* (New York: Julian Press, 1952); see also Helen Walker Puner, *Freud: His Life and His Mind* (New York: Howell Soskin, 1948); Hanns Sachs, *Freud: Master and Friend* (Cambridge: Harvard University Press, 1944); Ernest Jones, *The Life and Work of Sigmund Freud* (New York: Basic Books, 1953/55); Sigmund Freud, *The Origins of Psychoanalysis* (New York: Basic Books, 1954).

[52] S. Freud, *Civilization and Its Discontents* (London: Hogarth Press, 1930), p. 86.

[53] For a further discussion of this subject see pp. 71-73.

[54] Arthur Keith, *A New Theory of Evolution* (New York: Philosophical Library, 1948).

[55] P. R. David and L. S. Snyder, "Genetic Variability and Human Behavior," in J. H. Rohrer & M. Sherif (editors), *Psychology at the Crossroads* (New York: Harper & Bros., 1951), p. 71. See also Th. Dobzhansky and M. F. Ashley Montagu, "Natural Selection and the Mental Capacities of Mankind," *Science,* Vol. 105 (1947), pp. 587-590.

[56] For a survey of the evidence see M. F. Ashley Montagu, "Constitutional and Prenatal Factors in Infant and Child Health," in M. J. E. Senn (editor), *The Healthy Personality,* Josiah Macy, Jr., Foundation, pp. 148-210.

57 L. W. Sontag, "The Significance of Fetal Environmental Differences," *American Journal of Obstetrics and Gynecology,* Vol. 42 (1941), pp. 996-1003; L. W. Sontag, "Differences in Modifiability of Fetal Behavior and Physiology," *Psychosomatic Medicine,* Vol. 6 (1944), pp. 151-154.

58 For a helpful discussion of this subject see Clarence Leuba, *The Sexual Nature of Man,* "Doubleday Papers in Psychology" (New York: Doubleday, 1954), pp. 23-25.

59 For a full and authoritative survey of the evidence see John Bowlby, *Maternal Care and Mental Health* (Geneva & New York: World Health Organization, 1951).

60 See M. F. Ashley Montagu, *The Meaning of Love* (New York: Julian Press, 1953); D. A. Prescott, "The Role of Love in Human Development," *Journal of Home Economics,* Vol. 44 (1952), pp. 173-176; N. L. Foote, "Love," *Psychiatry,* Vol. 16 (1953), pp. 245-251; C. Caudwell, "Love," *Studies in a Dying Culture* (London: John Lane, 1938), pp. 129-157; Erich Fromm, *Man For Himself* (New York: Rinehart, 1947).

61 See Alfred Adler, *Social Interest: A Challenge to Mankind* (New York: Putnam, 1938); M. F. Ashley Montagu, *On Being Human* (New York: Abelard-Schuman, 1950), and *The Direction of Human Development* (New York: Harper & Bros., 1955).

62 L. Bender, "Genesis of Hostility in Children," *American Journal of Psychiatry,* Vol. 105 (1948), pp. 241-245. See also L. Bender, *Aggression, Hostility and Anxiety in Children* (Springfield, Ill.: Thomas, 1953).

63 A. H. Maslow, "Our Maligned Animal Nature," *Journal of Psychology,* Vol. 28 (1949), pp. 273-278.

64 *Ibid.,* pp. 275-276.

65 Karen Horney, *The Neurotic Personality of Our Time* (New York: Norton, 1937); E. Fromm, *Man For Himself* (New York: Rinehart, 1947); H. S. Sullivan, *The Interpersonal Theory of Psychiatry* (New York: Norton, 1954); I. Hendrick, "Instinct and Ego During Infancy," *Psychoanalytic Quarterly,* Vol. 11 (1942), pp. 33-59.

66 K. Menninger, *Love Against Hate* (New York: Harcourt Brace, 1942), p. 295.

67 R. Benedict, *Patterns of Culture* (New York: Mentor Books, 1936); Margaret Mead, *Coming of Age in Samoa* (New York: Mentor Books, 1928), *Sex and Temperament in Three Primitive Societies,* (New York: Mentor Books, 1935), and *And Keep Your Powder Dry* (New York: Morrow, 1942); C. Kluckhohn, H. Murray, and D. Schneider, *Personality: In Nature, Society, and Culture* (New York: Knopf, 1953); D. G. Haring (editor), *Personal Character and Cultural Milieu* (Syracuse, N. Y.: University of Syracuse Press, 1948); S. Stans-

feld Sargent and M. Smith (editors), *Culture and Personality* (New York: Viking Fund, 1949); F. L. K. Hsu (editor), *Aspects of Culture and Personality* (New York: Abelard-Schuman, 1954); John J. Honigmann, *Culture and Personality* (New York: Harper & Bros., 1954); Geoffrey Gorer, *Exploring English Character* (New York: Criterion Books, 1955); Margaret Mead and Martha Wolfenstein (editors), *Childhood in Contemporary Cultures* (Chicago: University of Chicago Press, 1955).

. [68] See George Gaylord Simpson, *The Meaning of Evolution* (New York: Mentor Books, 1953), and particularly H. G. Andrewartha and L. C. Birch, *The Distribution and Abundance of Animals* (Chicago: University of Chicago Press, 1954). See also M. F. Ashley Montagu, *Darwin, Competition, and Cooperation* (New York: Abelard-Schuman, 1952), and Th. Dobzhansky, *Evolution, Genetics, and Man* (New York: Wiley, 1955).

[69] By far the best modern edition of Malthus—a treasure in itself—is D. V. Glass, *Introduction to Malthus* (London: Watts, 1953).

[70] The passage is worth quoting in its entirety: "And the fact that all other creatures are aware of their own nature, some using speed, others swift flight, others swimming, whereas man alone knows nothing save by education—neither how to speak nor how to walk nor how to eat; in short the only thing he can do by natural instinct is to weep! Consequently there have been many who believed that it were best not to be born, or to be put away as soon as possible. On man alone of living creatures is bestowed grief, on him alone luxury, and that in countless forms and reaching every separate part of his frame; he alone has ambition, avarice, immeasurable appetite for life, superstition, anxiety about burial and even about what will happen when he is no more. No creature's life is more precarious, none has a greater lust for all enjoyments, a more confused timidity, a fiercer rage. In fine, all other living creatures pass their time worthily among their own species: we see them herd together and stand firm against other kinds of animals—fierce lions do not fight among themselves, the serpent's bite attacks not serpents, even the monsters of the sea and the fishes are only cruel against different species; whereas to man, I vow, most of his evils come from his fellow-man." Pliny, *Natural History*, Book VII (Translated by H. Rackham) (Cambridge: Harvard University Press, 1942), Vol. 2, pp. 509-511.

[71] V. G. Childe, *What Happened in History* (New York: Mentor Books, 1946); J. D. Clarkson and T. C. Cochran, *War As a Social Institution* (New York: Columbia University Press, 1941); R. Numelin, *The Beginnings of Diplomacy* (New York: Philosophical Library, 1950); M. F. Ashley Montagu, "'Race' and War," in the author's *Man's Most Dangerous Myth: The Fallacy of Race* (New York: Harper & Bros., 1952), pp. 182-208.

[72] E. S. Russell, *The Directiveness of Organic Activities* (New York: Cambridge University Press, 1945); E. B. Sinnott, *Cell and Psyche* (Chapel Hill: University of North Carolina Press, 1950).

[73] I. Suttie, *The Origins of Love and Hate* (New York: Julian Press, 1952), p. 31.

[74] L. G. Lowrey, "Personality Distortion and Early Institutional Care," *American Journal of Orthopsychiatry,* Vol. 10 (1940), pp. 576-585; D. M. Levy, "Primary Affect Hunger," *American Journal of Psychiatry,* Vol. 94 (1937), pp. 643-652; W. Goldfarb, "Effects of Psychological Deprivation in Infancy and Subsequent Stimulation," *American Journal of Psychiatry,* Vol. 102 (1945), pp. 18-33; R. Spitz, "Hospitalism," *The Psychoanalytic Study of the Child,* Vol. 1 (New York: International Universities Press, 1945), pp. 53-74; J. Bowlby, *Maternal Care and Mental Health* (Geneva & New York: World Health Organization, 1951); K. M. Banham, "The Development of Affectionate Behavior in Infancy," *Journal of Genetic Psychology,* Vol. 76 (1950), pp. 283-289; A. H. Maslow, *Motivation and Personality* (New York: Harper & Bros., 1954); M. Ribble, *The Rights of Infants* (New York: Columbia University Press, 1943).

[75] R. R. Sears, J. W. M. Whiting, V. Nowlis, and P. S. Sears, "Some Child-Rearing Antecedents of Aggression and Dependency in Young Children," *Genetic Psychology Monographs,* Vol. 47 (1953), pp. 135-278.

[76] F. Goldman-Eisler, "Breastfeeding and Character Formation," in C. Kluckhohn, H. A. Murray and D. Schneider, *Personality in Nature, Culture, and Society* (New York: Knopf, 1953), pp. 146-184.

[77] F. H. Richardson, *The Nursing Mother* (New York: Prentice-Hall, 1953); Niles Newton, *Maternal Emotions* (New York: Hoeber, 1955); M. F. Ashley Montagu, "Babies Should Be Born at Home," *Ladies Home Journal,* August 1955, pp. 52 ff.; M. Bevan-Brown, *The Sources of Love and Fear* (New York: Vanguard, 1950); M. P. Middlemore, *The Nursing Couple* (London: Cassell, 1941).

[78] J. L. Myres, *Political Ideas of the Greeks* (New York: Abingdon Press, 1927), p. 16.

[79] By "genotypically influenced potentialities" is meant those genetic potentialities which have already been influenced by the uterine environment.

[80] Ernst Cassirer, *An Essay on Man* (New York: Anchor Books, 1954).

[81] L. A. White, *The Science of Culture* (New York: Farrar, Straus, 1949).

[82] N. C. Tappen, "A Mechanistic Theory of Human Evolution," *American Anthropologist,* Vol. 55 (1953), pp. 605-607; M. F. Ashley Montagu, "Cultural and Physical Evolution," *American Anthropologist,*

Vol. 56 (1954), p. 290; W. Etkin, "Social Behavior and the Evolution of Man's Mental Faculties," *American Naturalist*, Vol. 88 (1954), pp. 129-142; M. R. A. Chance and A. P. Mead, "Social Behavior and Primate Evolution," *Symposia of the Society for Experimental Biology*, No. 7 (1953), pp. 395-439; C. S. Coon, "Human Races in Relation to Environment and Culture with Special Reference to the Influence of Culture Upon Genetic Changes in Human Populations," *Cold Spring Harbor Symposia on Quantitative Biology*, Vol. 15 (1950), pp. 247-258.

83 See Geoffrey Gorer, *Exploring English Character* (New York: Criterion Books, 1955).

84 In Johann G. Kohl, *England, Wales, and Scotland* (London: Chapman & Hall, 1844), p. 79.

85 See M. F. Ashley Montagu, "Isolation Versus Socialization" in the author's *The Direction of Human Development* (New York: Harper & Bros., 1955), pp. 266-287.

86 *Unesco Statement on Race*, 1950, Paragraph 9.

87 *Unesco Statement on the Nature of Race and Race Differences by Physical Anthropologists and Geneticists*, issued September 1952, Sections 5 and 6.

88 The supporting evidence will be found in Ashley Montagu, *Statement on Race*, 2nd ed. (New York: Abelard-Schuman, 1952), and in his *Man's Most Dangerous Myth: The Fallacy of Race*, 3rd ed. (New York: Harper & Bros., 1952). See also his *An Introduction to Physical Anthropology*, 2nd ed. (Springfield, Ill.: Thomas, 1951). See also the pamphlets on "race" published by Unesco.

89 Joseph A. de Gobineau, *Essai sur l'inégalité des races humaines* (Paris: 1853-55); H. S. Chamberlain, *Die Grundlagen des neunzehnten Jahrhunderts* (Berlin: 1899). For an excellent analysis of the racist writings and influence of Wagner see Leo Stein, *The Racial Thinking of Richard Wagner* (New York: Philosophical Library, 1950).

90 See Hannah Arendt, *The Origins of Totalitarianism* (New York: Harcourt Brace, 1951); Frederick Hertz, *Nationality in History and Politics* (London: Kegan Paul, 1944); and L. L. Snyder, *German Nationalism* (Harrisburg, Pa.: Stackpole, 1952).

91 See especially that remarkable book which, after fifty years, is still as readable and to the point as it was when it was first published, Jean Finot, *Les Préjugé des races* (Paris: 1905). English translation: *Race Prejudice* (Los Angeles: Zeitlin & Ver Brugge, 1945).

92 T. W. Adorno, E. Frenkel-Brunswik, D. J. Levenson, and R. Nevitt Sanford, *The Authoritarian Personality* (New York: Harper & Bros., 1950).

93 B. Bettelheim and M. Janowitz, "Prejudice," *Scientific American,* Vol. 183 (1950), p. 13. See also the same authors' *Dynamics of Prejudice* (New York: Harper & Bros., 1950).

94 Cesare Lombroso, *L'Uomo delinquente,* 1876.

95 K. F. Schluessler and D. R. Cressey, "Personality Characteristics of Criminals," *American Journal of Sociology,* Vol. 55 (1950), pp. 476-484.

96 In point of fact it is now known that there are no such things as atavistic characters. See M. F. Ashley Montagu, "The Concept of Atavism," *Science,* Vol. 87 (1938), pp. 462-463.

97 E. Ferri, *Sociologia criminale* (Torino: 1888); *Criminal Sociology* (Boston: 1917).

98 E. A. Hooton, *The American Criminal: An Anthropological Study* (Cambridge: Harvard University Press, 1939), and *Crime and the Man* (Cambridge: Harvard University Press, 1939).

99 E. A. Hooton, *Crime and the Man,* pp. 342-343.

100 *Ibid.,* p. 130.

101 *Ibid.,* p. 397.

102 For a more detailed criticism of Hooton's work see R. K. Merton and M. F. Ashley Montagu, "Crime and the Anthropologist," *American Anthropologist,* Vol. 42 (1940), pp. 384-408. See also W. A. Lessa, "An Appraisal of Constitutional Typologies," Memoir No. 62 of the American Anthropological Association, Vol. 45 (1943), p. 96.

103 J. Lange, *Verbrechen als Schicksal: Studien an Kriminellen Zwillingen* (Leipzig: 1929); English translation: *Crime and Destiny* (New York: Boni, 1930); A. M. Legras, *Psychose en Criminaliteit bij Tweelingen* (University of Utrecht, 1932); H. Kranz, *Lebensschicksale Krimineller Zwillinge* (Berlin: Springer, 1936); F. Stumpfl, *Die Ursprünge des Verbrechens, dargestellt am Lebenslauf von Zwillingen* (Leipzig: Thieme, 1936); A. J. Rosanoff, *et al.,* "Criminality and Delinquency in Twins," *Journal of Criminal Law and Criminology,* Vol. 24 (1934), pp. 923 ff.; A. J. Rosanoff, *et al., The Etiology of Child Behavior Difficulties, Juvenile Delinquency and Adult Criminality with Special Reference to Their Occurrence in Twins* (Sacramento: Moore, 1941).

104 H. H. Newman, *Multiple Human Births* (New York: Doubleday, 1940), p. 160.

105 *Ibid.*

106 W. C Reckless, *Criminal Behavior* (New York: McGraw-Hill, 1940), p. 186.

107 See M. F. Ashley Montagu, "The Biologist Looks at Crime," *Annals of the American Academy of Political and Social Science,* Vol. 217 (1941), pp. 46-57.

[108] The tables setting out these rates will be found on pp. 111-112.

[109] See Erich Fromm's recent discussion of this question in his book, *The Sane Society* (New York: Rinehart, 1955).

[110] For an extremely important proof of this, see Adelaide M. Johnson and S. A. Szurek, "Parental Sanction of Delinquency," *Journal of the American Medical Association,* Vol. 154 (1954); reprinted in *Child-Family Digest,* December 1955, pp. 72-81. See also Milton L. Barron, *The Juvenile in Delinquent Society* (New York: Knopf, 1954); Albert A. Cohen, *Delinquent Boys* (Glencoe, Ill.: Free Press, 1955); S. R. Slavson, *Re-educating the Delinquent* (New York: Harper & Bros., 1954); Arthur T. Collis and Vera E. Poole, *These Our Children* (Boston: Beacon Press, 1951).

[111] Herbert A. Bloch, *Disorganization* (New York: Knopf, 1952).

[112] A full description of Sheldon's methods and findings will be found in W. H. Sheldon, *The Varieties of Human Physique* (New York: Harper & Bros., 1940), *The Varieties of Human Temperament* (New York: Harper & Bros., 1942), *The Varieties of Delinquent Youth* (New York: Harper & Bros., 1949), *Atlas of Men* (New York: Harper & Bros., 1954).

[113] E. H. Sutherland, "Critique of Sheldon's *Varieties of Delinquent Youth,*" *American Journal of Sociology,* Vol. 57 (1951), pp. 10-13.

[114] W. H. Sheldon, *Varieties of Delinquent Youth,* pp. 842-843.

[115] *Ibid.,* pp. 744-745.

[116] *Ibid.,* p. 830.

[117] *Ibid.,* p. 879.